How to *die* well

A practical guide to
death, dying and loss

ROYAL
LONDON

Contents

Section Three

Saying goodbye

Good grief

Section Four

Epilogue

"Talking ab[out] most diffic[ult] in life mak[es] them so mu[ch]

out the

ult things

es living

ch easier"

Foreword

Death is a natural part of life – it's something that will happen to every one of us. But, somewhat strangely, it remains one of the last taboos.

Since the outbreak of the COVID-19 pandemic, the subject of death has never been so prominent. During a time of great difficulty and uncertainty, as a society we've looked to each other for support more than ever before. But despite it dominating the headlines and affecting our daily lives, we still find conversations about death incredibly hard.

Awkwardness, fear, sadness or discomfort can cause us to shy away, both from the topic itself and those who are dying or grieving. Thinking about death triggers an insight into grief for many, so it's understandable why people are reluctant to go there. We don't like to contemplate the end of our lives, or that of our loved ones, but I believe talking about death is critically important.

Royal London speaks to families when they're at their most vulnerable, often after losing a loved one. While everyone finds grief hard, the difficulty in dealing with the aftermath depends a lot on the preparation and discussions that people had beforehand. Conversations about death might be tough or uncomfortable, but getting your plans in place and letting your loved ones know your end-of-life wishes can actually give you a great deal of reassurance and peace of mind.

Through our conversations with our customers, we see the massively helpful impact that making financial plans in advance can have on those who are left behind. It can be the difference between a whole family coping financially or struggling for years. Planning to ensure your family's financial security might not be the most romantic gift, but it's perhaps one of the most loving things you can do.

Royal London wants to help people be better prepared for death – emotionally, practically and financially – and to encourage society to have more honest conversations about it. So we initiated the creation of this book to provide people with a practical guide to death, dying and loss. By approaching topics such as end-of-life preparations, funeral planning, saying goodbye to loved ones and coping with grief from a wealth of different perspectives, we hope to break down the taboo around death.

Situations like the COVID-19 outbreak are outside our control. But there are things within the control of every one of us that could make it easier for our loved ones when we die.

Barry O'Dwyer
CEO of Royal London

Introduction

"It's no surprise that most of us view dying as, basically, terrifying. But it doesn't have to be. Which is what this book is all about"

Death. The end (probably). The last great taboo. We don't want to think about it. We're reluctant to talk about it. Which is perfectly natural because of our powerlessness over it. But this is also behaviour akin to that popular myth of ostriches sticking their heads in the sand, since every single one of us, whoever we are, whatever our story, will die and be touched by death at some point.

Every day in the UK and Ireland, thousands of people die, expectedly and unexpectedly. In 2019, approximately 630,000 people died. Every single death touches numerous people — partners, family members, friends, colleagues, neighbours — which means that millions of us are hit by the shock of the news each year.

And while we seem happy to talk about sex or politics, to share our lives on social media, and to prepare for births and marriage, when it comes to death we're mostly silent and often totally unprepared. The thought of it is so terrifying, even alien, that we can barely find the words to voice how we feel.

Yet by not confronting death, we imbue it with power, real power, to frighten us. As humans in the 21st century, we're driven by perfection and avoid anything considered difficult — with death and dying at the top of that list. The harsh truth is, as a society, we're ill-equipped to deal with the death of others, let alone our own. The powerlessness, the lack of control, goes against our modern-day optimism that we're invincible. We think that medical technology can fix us, and if it can't, our own determination can.

It's no surprise that most of us view dying as, basically, terrifying. But it doesn't have to be. And that's what this book is all about. Inside, you'll find a practical (and sometimes humorous, because we need to laugh about this stuff, too) guide on how to prepare for the inevitable. There's information on funerals and the challenges of probate, the necessity of drafting your will and how to manage the estate (money, property, possessions, lifetime giving) of someone who has died. This book also covers the importance of arranging your own end-of-life care and good financial planning, and how to deal with bereavement and manage grief. A series of personal essays from leading personalities in the field offers ideas and insights into what death and dying mean, and how to understand and cope with it all. They cover everything from how to have that tender conversation with a dying relative to what the process of dying is actually like.

There's also a selection of interviews with people for whom death is truly a part of life. Flora Baker, the author of *The Adult Orphan Club*, speaks of the experience of losing both of her parents in her twenties; Yorkshire folk singer Ben Buddy Slack talks about his Swan Song Project, which pairs songwriters with people who are facing the end of their life so they can write a goodbye song as part of their legacy; and Judith Moran, director of Quaker Social Action, shares information about Down to Earth, the initiative the charity runs for those who are facing funeral poverty.

A subject rarely discussed, funeral poverty is a long-standing but relatively unknown problem, with large swathes of the population going into debt burying or cremating their loved ones, or finding themselves unable to arrange the funeral they wanted. From the price of ceremonies and burial or cremation plots to fulfilling people's end-of-life wishes, funeral expenses in the UK and Ireland are rising most years, while average incomes are not. Despite there being ways to keep costs down, more often than not, people are unaware of how to go about this. They might discover they don't have sufficient funds to cover these expenses, or haven't saved enough for their own funerals, which would alleviate the burden for those left behind. This book aims to help people prepare for death as best they can, financially, practically and emotionally.

Because dying well is important, right? In continuing to avoid talking about death or dealing with the facts of it, we're leaving ourselves and those closest to us open to many problems when the end comes.

We know in our hearts that love and loss will always co-exist, that one does not happen without the other, just like light cannot exist without dark. Loss through death is intrinsic to our collective human experience. And in order to live truly, to experience life fully, we have to be able to accept that.

Before you

Section One

re

go

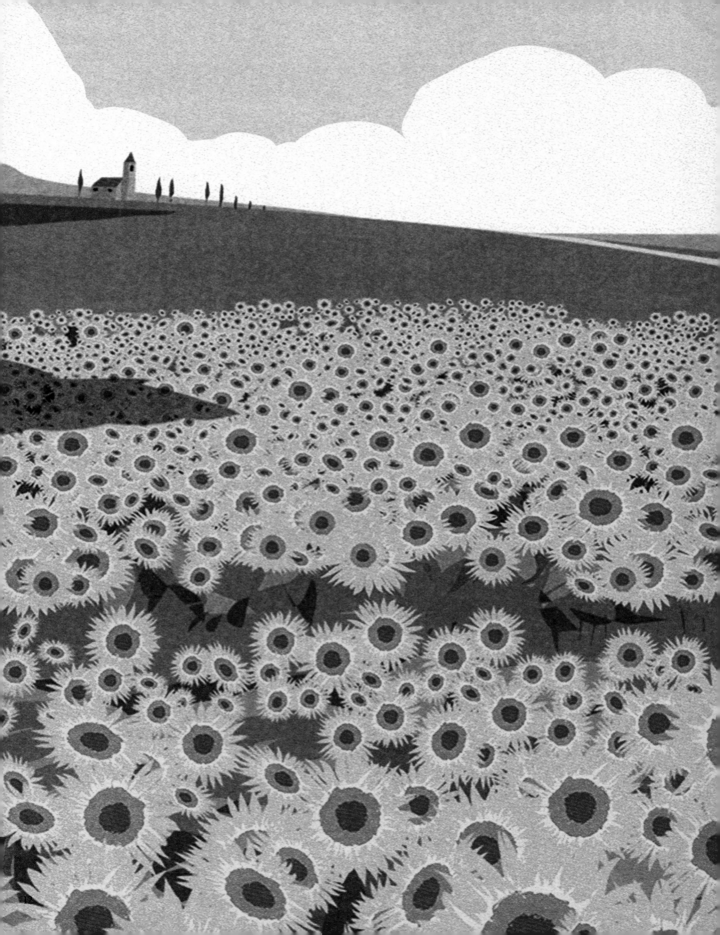

Death? Let's talk
Rhik Samadder

The writer and actor shares
how the sudden death of
his father turned a lifetime
obsession with mortality
into a heartfelt need to
talk openly about grief

I've been talking about death for as long as I can remember. The knowledge of death clouded even my childhood, or lack of knowledge, to be precise. For Death is the Great Uncertain, the dark into which the light of reason cannot shine. I could not stop talking about the fact it was coming, every day, to anyone who would listen – a bit like how I was about the movie *Arachnophobia*, which terrified me too, yet I rewatched it every Saturday, right after *Gladiators*.

Perhaps such a fixation is odd in a child. I used to have panic attacks contemplating my own annihilation at night, then run to my mother, asking if I was really going to die. This is every parent's nightmare. Especially when the child keeps it up into their teens – knocking on their bedroom door in the middle of the night, totally naked, begging for reassurance about mortality. I can't remember her response, but it may have been, "What time is it?" (Answer: later than you think.) By university, I was ruining every party by pulling out my trick: reeling off a litany of cancer stats, comorbidities, suicide factors, final words. I was a walking actuarial life table, which meant most people didn't want to hang out with me for longer than eight minutes. "Social isolation carries a 30% higher risk of early death," I would whimper into a supermarket whisky and off-brand cola, alone.

Then, in my mid-twenties, my father died. He had a short illness at Christmas and in January he was gone. My obsessive wondering about what lies beyond was suddenly answered by a painful, real-world initiation into grief. I found that I needed to talk more than ever, but from a different place. There's not much to say about death as an experience, because it is a mystery beyond language. But the experience of grieving – it is vital to talk about that. We need a place to put our feelings of loneliness and anger and incomprehension, our depression and exhaustion. The healthiest place is in words with friends, by which I don't mean the online, Scrabble-type game. Although they would be worth a lot of points.

We don't talk about death much in this country, I think because we wrongly believe there aren't enough jokes in it. We avoid the recently bereaved, as if their condition were contagious. We don't know what to say to them, we tell ourselves. Let's give them space. Reconnect after a little time has passed. I can tell you now, it'll be too late by then. I can tell you that enduring relationships are not made in peace time, they are forged and strengthened by the war. Show up, on the front line. The truth is that if you speak from the heart, you can say almost anything

to a bereaved person. Don't worry that they will be repulsed by your awkward words; more likely they will shelter in them, like the lee of a rock in a storm. They may do so privately and never tell. But it's always worth taking a few seconds or offering company if you can.

I will never forget those who sat with me or messaged in an ongoing way after my father's death. It helped them too, I think. To talk about death is to face reality, and there's no other way to grow. It wasn't all death chat either. Mostly it was stupid stuff. Debating the difference between jam and marmalade. (The presence of citrus.) Betting which member of Destiny's Child would have the biggest solo career. (Michelle Williams, playing the long game.) Deciding whether it would be better to have feet for hands, or hands for feet. (Obviously the first; you'd win the World Cup single-handedly.) Knowing that I *could* talk about my grief if needed, how lonely and afraid I felt at times, meant I didn't have to exclusively feel those things. It meant there wasn't an elephant in the room.

I no longer talk about death every day. A couple of times a week, sure. It passes the time in a post office queue like nothing else. For now, I'm busy with other things: matcha lattes, pigeon welfare, ping-pong videos on YouTube. Life. Nevertheless, I take care to hang onto the gifts my obsession gave me. Lessons in perspective, true value, appreciating moments and choosing one's existence. A short life embraced wholeheartedly, nothing held back, is infinitely richer than a long one lived in fear. If the price of a go on this magical ride – with all its exhilaration and mystery – is getting off eventually to give someone else a turn, well. It's still worth it. Those spiders can go to hell, though.

Preparing for death:
your checklist

We don't live in a culture where talking about death, or even thinking about it, comes easy. That's what can make it even more difficult to take stock and decide what's best for you when it comes to the end of your life. In order to help you with the process, we've compiled a list of things to consider in your planning. Thinking about your final wishes in advance will make handling your estate easier, and therefore less painful, for your family and loved ones. It'll help them avoid having to guess what you would have wanted while they're grieving.

The reflective bit

Before you get bogged down with the nitty-gritty of getting your affairs in order – someone's got to do it and, for practical reasons, it ought to be you – you should think about how you want to approach death and what it means to you. How would you ideally like your final months to play out? What, apart from your assets, do you want to pass on to your loved ones? Besides a funeral, how do you want to say goodbye before you're gone, if you have the chance?

Making a difference

If you had a lot of moral convictions in life, how can you continue to honour those principles after death? Do some research into charitable causes that you could donate to via your will. Or, if you're a bit short on assets, think about suggesting that those attending your funeral donate to a cause that's close to your heart instead of buying flowers. Additionally, if you live in England, Scotland or Wales (where there's an opt-out system), your organs will be donated upon your death, helping others to keep on living after you. In Northern Ireland and the Republic of Ireland you can opt in to donating.

What you leave behind

Take stock of what you have and how or whether you want those things to live on. And think about where value lies in their physical, intellectual and emotional forms, rather than in terms of monetary worth. To whom will you bequeath your carefully curated book, record or rare cactus collection? Will you write down your family recipes so you can pass them on to the next generation (or your cuisine-curious best friend)? Should you start posting your pearls of wisdom on a public blog, so that your thoughts and turns of phrase are available to all, even after your death?

The logistics

After you've had plenty of contemplation, it's time to put your newly found realisations to good use. Death comes with a lot of paperwork, so get ready to flex your admin muscles.

Life insurance

The challenging thing about preparing for death is, no matter how organised we are, we still won't know when the end is coming. To mitigate the effects of a sudden death, life insurance can be a good choice. Particularly important if you have children or other dependants, or support a long-term partner, life cover can prevent your loved ones from being stuck with the burden of repayments they can't afford or dealing with the sudden financial shock that comes from losing the household's primary earner.

There are plenty of easy-to-use online tools that will help you compare different offers or providers, depending on how much you're willing to spend, your age, health and the job you do, and the kind of coverage you're looking for. Seeking the help of a financial adviser can also be valuable. They'll be able to recommend suitable products based on your personal situation and needs, giving you peace of mind that you're prepared.

Getting your estate in order – what to do

Select a trusted executor

Make a shortlist of the different people in your life and who you can rely on to handle your affairs after you die. Once you've decided, and after discussing it with them first, name your top candidates as executors (more on writing that up later), who will carry out the wishes outlined in your will. If there's no one who can be your executor, you can name a government official (called a public trustee) instead.

Valuing your assets

In order to help your executors, you may want to work out how much you're worth. This includes calculating your debts against any money you have tied up in bank accounts, savings, PayPal accounts, pensions, life insurance policies, stocks, shares and cryptocurrency holdings. If you're a homeowner, you should also value your property – either officially via a property surveyor with Royal Institution of Chartered Surveyors (RICS) accreditation, or by "guess-timation", through scoping out similar properties in your area using sites such as Zoopla.

Your will

If you want to minimise stress and make sure your wishes are adhered to after your death, this one is important, so listen up! Firstly, engage a lawyer – you can write your will yourself, but it'll need to be signed by two witnesses over the age of 18 in order for it to be legally sound (in Scotland you just need one witness over the age of 16). In your will, you should express who you want your estate to go to, who should look after your dependants (if you have any), who your executors are and what should happen if the people you want to benefit from your will end up dying before you do. If your financial situation is a bit more complicated, you should almost certainly seek the advice of a legal professional. Remember to also keep your will up to date – it will become invalid if you get married after it's written, for example (unless you live in Scotland).

Letter of wishes

A letter of wishes is a non-legally-binding document that accompanies your will, further clarifying your wishes. You might want to include details of who to notify in the event of your death, the kind of funeral you want or any advice to guardians on how you would like your children to be brought up.

Your funeral

Remember: it's good to talk, so as well as including your funeral wishes in your letter, have the conversation about what kind of funeral you want directly with your loved ones to take the guess-work out of it. To relieve the financial burden on them, consider paying for it in advance, if you can afford to.

Death folder

This is a digital or physical folder containing important documents in the case of your death. It'll likely hold a copy of your will and letter of wishes, as well as insurance and pension policies, contact details for your solicitor and the executors of your will, and bank account details. Make sure you let somebody know where this folder is.

What are my end-of-life wishes?

"All of us will be intimate with death at least once. When we demystify death and encourage critical thinking, research and debate about it, we will better learn how to support one another in this unavoidable part of life"
Kathy Kortes-Miller, *Talking About Death Won't Kill You: The Essential Guide to End-of-Life Conversations*

Most of us fear death, that's only natural. But part of getting over this fear, or at least making dying more acceptable, is thinking about it in the first place and, moreover, preparing for it. If, for example, you've discussed what you want to happen with your family and those close to you, and have sorted out your affairs, you're likely to be far less fearful when the time comes. And perhaps your loved ones will be, too.

To that end, ensuring your end-of-life wishes are understood by those close to you, and indeed, are protected, is crucial. First and most importantly, make a will (see page 28). Afterwards, take all of the practical steps that are necessary, such as writing a letter of wishes to be included with your will and submitting it to a solicitor for safekeeping or storing it at home in a secure and fireproof place. This will ensure that these wishes will be taken into account by the executors of your will – your solicitor or whoever you've designated.

The letter of wishes might include things you'd like to say to certain people or things you'd like to happen after you've died. For instance, you could provide instructions for what you want to happen at your funeral or memorial – or even state that you don't want one at all! The main point here is that your wishes are made clear and don't conflict with your will, though the letter is not legally binding like a will.

Of course, this also means you're going to have to think about exactly what you want, which can be difficult. Ideally, sit down with your loved ones to discuss everything with them so they know, too. This is something that will be particularly helpful if you live far away from them or are ageing, or if it comes

to a point where you've become incapacitated by a terminal illness, or mental deterioration, and need end-of-life care and decisions to be made on your behalf. An advance decision, also known as a living will, is legally binding. It involves such issues as deciding what treatment you receive – for example, whether or not you'd want to receive life-sustaining care. It's advisable to consult a lawyer in these cases and make sure they're informed of any advance decisions you make. You can also set up an ongoing power of attorney, giving someone you trust the legal authority to make decisions (financial, health/welfare) on your behalf.

On a practical note, when you're arranging to sit down with your loved ones to discuss things, you may find the below guidance helpful:

○ Choose a time and place where you won't be disturbed or rushed, so you feel you can say all you want to.

○ Give them advance notice so they're not taken by surprise.

○ Make some notes beforehand so you cover everything.

○ Don't be embarrassed if you get emotional. Be honest and talk about all your feelings, not just the positive ones.

Nothing about discussing or organising your end-of-life wishes is easy, but if you follow this blueprint it might just be a more positive experience than a negative one, and you'll be able to ensure that what you want to happen does happen. There's a lot to be said for that sort of peace of mind.

Don't have a will? You're not the only one
More than half (54%) of adults in the UK don't have a will, with 5.4 million people being unsure of how to make one. For parents with children under the age of 18 (or 16 in Scotland) it's especially important to draw up a will, as it determines who will raise your offspring in the event of your death. It's also necessary to keep your will updated – a good example, as already mentioned, is that pre-existing wills become invalid when you get married, unless you live in Scotland.

What am I supposed to leave behind when I die?

There are so many answers to this question it's hard to know where to begin. Lots of evidence of a life well lived, perhaps; good memories for all who love you; as few debts as possible; completed arrangements for your funeral; and ideally, no awful secrets that will come out after you've died.

You may want to send your loved ones on a round-the-world adventure to scatter your ashes, or on a darker note, you may feel like planning a series of unfortunate events to befall your enemies from beyond the grave. It's been done!

Whatever your thoughts on the matter, spending a little time putting your affairs in order before saying farewell to this world can save a large amount of time and money for those you leave behind.

To do this, enlist a lawyer, make a will and check your executors are happy to take on the task. Write a list of your assets, from bank accounts to obscure shareholdings (don't forget that cryptocurrency you were convinced to buy in 2016), and put all the relevant documents in one file – your death folder (see page 17). These could be property deeds, insurance policies, mortgage information, birth and marriage certificates. Remember, even if you don't own a home, a company or a Damien Hirst painting, it doesn't mean you don't have anything important to leave behind. For instance, an employee benefit in many companies is death in service cover, which can pay out a lump sum of two to four times your salary, or more, if you die while on the payroll – something worth thinking about and including details of in your folder.

Once you've assembled your death folder, don't forget to nominate beneficiaries and explain where all the relevant documents can be found. That's pretty much all the formal stuff. But what about the informal stuff?

You might want to create a personal website where your legacy can be preserved online – or leave instructions for someone to do it for you. You might want to make video or voice recordings for your loved ones, write letters to friends and family expressing your feelings and thoughts, keep a diary to be read after your death, or put together a memory box of important objects or mementos you wish others to have. There's more on all that in our chapter on saying goodbye (page 104).

At the same time, you might not want the private contents of your email inbox or WhatsApp messages to be seen by anyone – in which case, arrange for someone you trust to delete your accounts when you've gone (see page 128 for more details).

Your legacy, what you leave behind, is something entirely personal to you. Perhaps you don't want to be remembered at all. Either way, make sure to leave clear instructions. In the meantime, live well!

> **Don't bin your bitcoin**
> Researchers estimate that as much as 3.8 million bitcoin, worth up to £22.8 billion (€25.5 billion), has been carried to the grave with their holders, due to there being no explanation in their wills of how to retrieve their cryptocurrency.

But how can I leave behind some good?

"Don't sink into the oblivion of ages. Give humanity something to remember you by"

"[The gene] leaps from body to body down the generations, manipulating body after body in its own way and for its own ends, abandoning a succession of mortal bodies before they sink in senility and death. [...] When we have served our purpose we are cast aside. But genes are denizens of geological time. [...] Genes, like diamonds, are forever"
Richard Dawkins, *The Selfish Gene*

Don't sink into the oblivion of ages. Give humanity something to remember you by, whether it be a work of art, "loadsamoney" or simply the sheer force of your personality.

With a bit of luck, you'll have spent your life doing some good already – supporting good causes and spreading happiness and positivity among people you meet. Heck, you may even work in a field where the whole purpose is to do good – you may be a doctor or nurse, climate-crisis activist, bin man or woman... There are countless other worthy professions, of course, and naturally, job or no job, the way you live your life also contributes to the good you leave behind. So you might think you've done your bit, even if that sounds a little mean-spirited. The thing is, there's a lot we can do to ensure we leave behind some good when we finally pop our clogs, and why not? After all, we're part of thousands of years of positive human history and progress, the same species working together to build a better future. And most religious beliefs advise giving as well as taking, doing unto others as you would have them do unto you, being generous – and that you reap what you sow.

Leaving some good – beyond helping your loved ones with whatever financial support you can – isn't that hard or costly. For a start, have you considered organ donation? As mentioned, if you're a resident of the Republic of Ireland and Northern Ireland, you need to opt in to become an organ donor, while in England, Scotland and Wales, everyone is now an organ donor under the law unless you opt out. If you want to go even further, you can donate your body to science, thereby allowing medical students and researchers to benefit, and hopefully humanity, too, thanks to the great life-saving discoveries those students and researchers could make.

Next on the list are charitable donations. Many people leave a portion of their estate to charity or to a cause they believe in. There are so many it might be difficult to choose one, but for the record, cancer and animal charities, along with children's hospitals, are the most popular. You could create your own trust, charity or foundation and leave it with the funds to do good in your name for a cause you care about – for example, planting trees in the Amazon rainforest or even your local park. Whatever you decide on, you can be assured this sort of legacy will benefit people, and the options are many and varied.

Leaving behind some good doesn't have to be financially focused, though. You might have a collection of records, vintage magazines, unusual seashells, valuable stamps or a library of first-edition James Joyce novels you could leave to a museum/school/university for the benefit of many.

Responsible financial investment is also becoming increasingly important to people, giving them some peace of mind that the planet might survive the next global catastrophe. By investing responsibly you can use your money to help make the world a better place in the future, after you're gone. You could invest your pension into a sustainable fund that focuses on renewable energy, for instance, to make sure that your money is being used to manage sustainable causes – that way, you'll be taking care of the next generation from beyond the grave.

Do I really need life insurance?

"If you're someone with a mortgage, a family and kids, have debts owing or you're the main earner and don't have a substantial amount of savings, the payout your loved ones would get if you were to die could be a lifeline"

"A policy of life insurance is the cheapest and safest mode of making a certain provision for one's family"
Benjamin Franklin, 1769

Before you start thinking about funeral plans and how you'd say goodbye to your loved ones, it's important to get the paperwork sorted. First stop: write or check your will, and appoint executors. Next? Check your life insurance policy or consider taking one out if you haven't done so already.

With life insurance, you make a monthly payment to an insurer and in return they agree to pay out a set amount to your dependants in the event of your untimely death. If you're fit and healthy and just starting out in your working life with little cash and lots to sort out, it's an expense you might think you can avoid. But life insurance isn't something that just becomes relevant in your silver years – it's important to consider at key landmarks in life, such as buying a house with a partner or starting a family. If you're someone with a mortgage, a family and kids, have debts owing or you're the main earner and don't have a substantial amount of savings, the payout your loved ones would get if you were to die could be a lifeline. Life cover can also be valuable for those without a large debt to repay. For a young couple who are renting, for instance, a death may make those rental commitments or fixed-cost bills impossible to meet for the remaining partner.

So, if family members or loved ones you're going to leave behind would suffer financially if you died – maybe they will struggle to pay the mortgage or bills – then it's a good idea to get some sort of life cover overall and let your dependants know the details of your policy. Remember, some companies provide life cover as part of their benefits package, so it's also worth checking this with your employer.

How much cover do you need? Good question. Generally, the answer is as much as you'd need to fill any financial gap left by your death. You should ensure that your outstanding debts would be paid off, including your mortgage and any loans, and that you think about how much cover you might need to pay for things such as childcare, school fees or higher-education costs. It's also important to consider flexibility within your insurance policy, to allow you to review it as your situation or family life changes over time. Enlisting the help of a financial adviser can be valuable, as they can look at your personal situation and assess what kind of cover you need. But remember: the bigger the payout you want, the higher your premiums will be, so you need to factor in affordability.

Which brings us to the cost. It doesn't have to be expensive – life insurance is a particularly competitive market. What you pay depends on your age, health, lifestyle, smoking habit, policy length and amount of money you want to cover. Typically, if you're younger, fitter and healthier, insurance is cheaper. If you're a smoker, overweight, older, a drinker or just unhealthy, it could be more expensive.

Oh, and before we forget, it might also be pricier if you have a risky job – think armed forces, professional deep-sea diver or sportsperson. In that case, either consider taking up knitting instead or find a specialist broker who can help you.

Rome's funerals weren't planned in a day
The concept of life insurance goes as far back as ancient Rome, where low-income individuals made regular contributions to burial clubs. Eventually, this money would go towards the cost of their funeral to ensure they had a dignified send-off.

Do I really need a will?

"Wills are uncanny and electric documents. They lie dormant for years and then spring to life when their author dies, as if death were rain. Their effect on those they enrich is never negligible, and sometimes unexpectedly charged. They thrust living and dead into a final fierce clasp of love or hatred"
Janet Malcolm, *The New Yorker*

It's fairly simple. If you own anything of value – whether that's savings or a property – and you want to decide who inherits what you own, then you'll want to make a will. This is a written legal document that details how you would like your estate to be distributed. If you have children under the age of 18, you can also use your will to name a legal guardian (or guardians) to look after them if something were to happen to you and make provisions for their care – just make sure you check this with your preferred guardians beforehand. A will is usually accompanied by a letter of wishes, which can include things like the type of funeral service or memorial you'd like and advice for guardians on how you'd like your children to be raised.

If you're young with no dependants, have little money and own nothing of value, you can probably manage without one – unless you're attached to what happens to your body. If so, a will stating your preferences and signed by you (the testator) and two witnesses (you only need one in Scotland) is paramount if you want to make sure your executors know your wishes. According to UK death experts Farewill, one person specified in their will that their ashes should not be flushed down the toilet under any circumstances.

A will can also be used to divide assets among friends and family (and sometimes pets, if a trust is set up to pay for their care), and to make donations to charity. Once it's written, it's a good idea to pay to have it registered and stored by a solicitor for safekeeping,

or you can simply register it with the National Will Register (although this doesn't exist in Scotland) or the Irish Will Register in Ireland, or even keep it at home (as long as it's somewhere secure); just make sure to inform someone it exists. While you don't have to pay a lawyer to help with your will, there are advantages to having one. They can provide basic inheritance tax planning advice and help you avoid mistakes. Plus, because they're regulated, your beneficiaries would be able to complain to the ombudsman, or Legal Complaints Commission in Scotland, if things go wrong.

A will also helps stop disputes happening over what you leave behind and makes your final wishes clear for the avoidance of any doubt, as well as helping to manage the amount of inheritance tax your estate will pay to the state when you die. If you pass away without a will, you're treated as an intestate person and your assets are allocated under the rules of intestacy, which basically means the law of the land will decide who gets what, and only spouses or civil partners, children and some other close relatives can inherit assets. It's worth noting that, in Scotland, whether you have a will or not, your children or spouse can never legally be disinherited.

These old-fashioned laws may cause issues if there's a second marriage or you lived with someone but didn't marry. Don't worry, though, there are plenty of solicitors that specialise in wills and interitance tax issues who will be able to help – so get will writing!

A royal privilege
If you live in the UK and die without a will and have no living beneficiaries, under the rules of intestacy your estate will go to the Crown and the Treasury will be responsible for dealing with it.

Inheritance tax... sounds complicated

"Remember there's nothing wrong with arranging your financial affairs to reduce your own and your family's tax liabilities. You won't regret it!"

Put very simply, inheritance tax is a tax due to the state on the estate of a person who has died. Also known as capital acquisitions tax in Ireland, or the "gift tax", it ain't a fun subject, and it can get pretty complicated, so it's worth being as informed as possible if you don't want to end up letting the taxman have more of your cash than due.

Under the 2020/2021 tax year rules, an individual in the UK can pass on up to £325,000 of their estate without their heirs having to pay any inheritance tax. This is called the nil rate band (NRB). However, if your estate is going to a spouse or civil partner, there's normally no tax to pay – plus, when you die, any of your unused NRB is added to their allowance, giving them a total of up to £650,000. On top of this, there's the residence nil rate band (RNRB). This means the first £175,000 of your property's value is exempt from inheritance tax if it's being passed on to direct descendants – that is, children or grandchildren. As with the NRB, any unused RNRB can be passed onto a spouse or civil partner. For people whose assets exceed these thresholds, inheritance tax is usually charged at 40%. In Ireland, there are different thresholds, tax rates and rules that apply to gifts or inheritances (there's more information about this online at *revenue.ie*) and capital acquisitions tax is charged at 33% for people who exceed these thresholds.

There are further reliefs alongside spousal exemption, including an annual exemption (£3,000 per year) and gifts for weddings or civil ceremonies (£5,000 for a child or £2,500 for a grandchild per year). There's also a small gifts allowance each year, which allows you to give as many gifts of up to £250 per person as you want, as long as you haven't used another exemption for those people. You can give away more than this, including money, property, possessions and shares, and pay no inheritance tax as long as you live for at least seven years after making the gift. In addition, you can give unlimited gifts if they're from your regular income and don't reduce your standard of living. Other reliefs include business property relief and agricultural relief.

Want to avoid inheritance tax? Move to Russia! The countries with the highest rates of inheritance tax are Japan, where it reaches up to 55%, and South Korea, where the top bracket sits at 50%. On the flip side, nations such as China, India and Russia have no inheritance tax at all.

The executors of the will/estate are responsible for ensuring that inheritance tax is paid (using money released from the estate), but the beneficiaries aren't, unless they're also the executors. However this is common. And this means the estate's value must be estimated, submitted and sometimes evidenced. Once all of that is done, probate via a court order can be granted. Working out the value of the estate can be done by the executors but, if possible, it's worth getting a probate solicitor or tax adviser involved – there are countless forms to fill in, calculations to be made and thresholds to understand. It's also a good idea to enlist the help of an expert when writing your will, too, as they'll be able to advise on minimising the amount of inheritance tax to be paid. For instance, in the UK, if you choose to leave some money to a charity, that donation won't be taxed, and if the donation amounts to 10% of the net estate, then that reduces inheritance tax to 36%.

Probate and inheritance tax issues can take time. Delays are prevalent. But if you do your homework, prepare your affairs in advance, and take professional advice or appoint a solicitor, the whole thing can be managed prudently and efficiently. Remember, there's nothing wrong with arranging your financial affairs to reduce your own and your family's tax liabilities. You won't regret it!

What will I do if I can't afford end-of-life care?

"How people die remains in the memory of those who live on" **Dame Cicely Saunders, founder of the modern hospice movement**

Many terminal or long-term sicknesses can be extremely painful and debilitating, and it might actually be months or years before such a disease finally takes you. With illnesses such as dementia, Alzheimer's, Parkinson's and multiple sclerosis, you may also require round-the-clock care from others, as you'll be unable to complete basic tasks. And you may not want that burden to fall solely on your loved ones' shoulders, or you may not have any loved ones.

It's pretty dark stuff, really. Still, compared to the rest of the world, and across the population as a whole, the UK and Ireland are good places to die. In fact, a 2015 report by the Economist Intelligence Unit rated the UK as the best place to die out of 80 countries, with Ireland ranking number four (after Australia and New Zealand).

What does that translate to in reality? It means that in most of the above cases of end-of-life care – that is, care for patients considered to specifically be in the last stage of their lives – the NHS, or the HSE (Health Service Executive) in Ireland, will meet your basic care needs. Palliative care, as this is known, which includes the management of pain and other symptoms and provision of psychological, social, spiritual and practical support, is free. Following assesment, the NHS/HSE, your local council or your hospice (hospitals specifically dedicated to people who are dying) will provide nurses and carers who come to your home and equipment such as hospital beds and wheelchairs, as well as all the pain-management medicine and support you may need.

It's unlikely to be round-the-clock care if you wish to stay at home, although it would be in a hospice.

Such care isn't always conditional on how much money you have, although it can be means-tested, especially in the UK. Often, however, it's based simply on the complexity of your medical condition. So, unless you want specialist private care or want to end your life in a luxury mountain retreat in Switzerland, in the case of terminal illnesses, you won't have an issue affording end-of-life care.

"Compared to the rest of the world, the UK and Ireland are good places to die"

When will I die?

Whether you care to admit it or not, at some point you've reflected on when you might die. For some of us, it's just an occasional, fleeting thought, but for others it can be a recurring question. For better or worse, there's no magic death clock that can give you an exact answer, but a lot of scientific research has been done to give us a better understanding of when our time might be up.

Life expectancy in the UK over two centuries (years)

Late 1700s
39

Today
81.4

Life expectancy in the UK today (years)

Women
83.6

Men
79.9

Life expectancy for the homeless is shockingly low in England. In 2018, the Office for National Statistics (ONS) reported that the average age for homeless people to die in England and Wales was 45 years for men and 43 for women.

In the UK, life expectancy has increased greatly over the past 250 years, thanks to better housing, education, sanitation and medical advancements. While the average life expectancy hovered around 39 years in the late 1700s, it is now 81.4 according to the UN.

In 2019, figures from the Department of Health indicated that, in Ireland, the average life expectancy at birth is 80.4 years for men and 84 for women. In England and Wales, according to the The King's Fund, it's 79.9 and 83.6, respectively, while in Northern Ireland the average is 78.5 and 82.3.

According to the Central Statistics Office, malignant cancers were the main cause of death in Ireland in 2019, followed by circulatory disease. In the UK, it's currently dementia (including Alzheimer's). Meanwhile, Bupa reports that almost 80,000 people die annually from smoking-related diseases in the UK. It goes on to say that smoking can reduce your life expectancy by up to 10 years, and after you reach the age of 40, each additional year that you keep up the habit reduces your life expectancy by another three months.

Generally, women tend to have a longer life expectancy than men, but this hasn't always been the case. In the 19th century, men lived longer than them. Different factors, such as biology, behaviour and environment, have contributed to this shift, with medical advancements, particularly regarding childbirth, giving women the upper hand. Research from 2020 (Our World in Data) shows that, in Russia, women live 10 years longer than men on average. The high mortality rate among men is theorised to be caused by alcohol poisoning, smoking and stress.

Despite the commonly held belief that living by the sea increases your life expectancy, inhabitants of the seaside town of Blackpool have a significantly low life expectancy rate: 74.5 years for men and 79.5 for women.

If you're a Londoner, life expectancy at birth is 80.7 years for men and 84.5 for women. Compared with the northeast, which has the lowest life expectancy in England, this represents a difference of 2.8 years for both sexes.

The ONS reports that the lowest healthy life expectancy for women in England was found to be in Nottingham, at an average of 54.2 years.

The United Nations Development Programme released a study in 2019 that showed the nations with the highest life expectancy in the world are Hong Kong (84.7 years), Japan (84.5) and Singapore (83.8). Ireland came in 16th, while the UK ranked 29th.

In *Population Change and Trends in Life Expectancy*, a 2018 survey by Public Health England, it was reported that, since 2011, the rate of growth for life expectancy has slowed for both men and women.

In 2020, the National Records of Scotland reported that the average life expectancy in the country is 77.1 years for men and 81.1 for women. However, while this is the lowest life expectancy of all the countries in the UK, Scottish men spend a higher proportion of their life in good health compared with their counterparts in England, Wales and Northern Ireland.

Your bucket list

Whether it's climbing Mount Everest or trying every cocktail on the menu in your favourite bar, there's no right or wrong way to do a bucket list. Put simply, it's a wish list of everything you'd like to do before you die. It's impossible to know when you might go, so there's no time like the present to make your dreams happen and live your best life. This is a space to write down anything that you might like to experience before your time is up.

20 things to do before you die

☐ _____   ☐ _____

☐ _____   ☐ _____

☐ _____   ☐ _____

☐ _____   ☐ _____

☐ _____   ☐ _____

☐ _____   ☐ _____

☐ _____   ☐ _____

☐ _____   ☐ _____

☐ _____   ☐ _____

☐ _____   ☐ _____

Interview with
Louise Winter
Funeral director

The founder of Poetic Endings,
a contemporary and ethical
funeral directors based in
London, shares her thoughts
on how the funeral industry
is changing for the better

Louise Winter is a progressive funeral director and the founder of Poetic Endings, a London-based funeral service that offers "thoughtful, creative and affordable funerals".

She is also a co-director of Life. Death. Whatever., an initiative that aims to shake up the dialogue surrounding death and dying. Her new book *We All Know How This Ends* was written with the equally progressive Anna Lyons, an end-of-life doula.

Q **What exactly does the term "progressive funeral director" mean?**

A It means that we're not like other funeral directors! More conventional funeral directors often have a set way of working and don't really know how to go outside that. They're more [traditional] and can be inflexible in their approach. The term "progressive funeral director" demonstrates a different attitude and approach towards funerals. That doesn't necessarily mean turning funerals into parties and having big celebrations of life, it means bringing a different skill set to the role – creativity, emotional intelligence and more flexibility. [At Poetic Endings] we like to think that we understand the meaning of ritual and ceremony, but also that it needs to be relevant to our times. Ritual without relevance is just a formality. We try to incorporate a creative process into the funeral service we offer, which I hope serves bereaved people of today and tomorrow.

Q **Why do you think we still have a Victorian-esque image of what funerals should look like in the UK – the top hats and horse-drawn hearses?**

A Victorian funerals are a bit of a myth perpetuated by the funeral industry. The industry is not that old – the Victorian way of doing funerals didn't necessarily involve funeral directors. Many people arranged funerals themselves and cared for the person who had died at home in the front room. During the wake, everyone came to visit the person to make absolutely sure they were dead before they were buried. Then, times changed and society became more squeamish about death, for various reasons – we had two world wars, the NHS was introduced, we had a major flu epidemic, we learnt more about germs and medicine, religion became less relevant and set beliefs in there being afterlife became less common. All of these things came together to mean that death was something

people didn't want in their homes any more. It became this thing that people wanted to keep at a distance, as far away as possible. Funeral directors did exist but they weren't as commercial as they are now. They were often builders or joiners who were asked to make coffins. They quickly saw an opportunity to turn something that used to belong to family and friends into a commercial process. That's how the high street funeral director became the norm. That continued to the point where we are now, where the government has had to step in to investigate the funeral industry due to questionable practices and exploitative behaviour.

Q **Please tell us a bit about your book *We All Know How This Ends*.**

A I started the project Life. Death. Whatever. with my colleague Anna Lyons, who works with people who are facing the end of their life. Life. Death. Whatever. is all about coming together to help everyone to have a more empowered approach to whatever they're going through. Whether they're facing difficult conversations with their doctor or are imminently arranging a funeral, they need to know what questions ought to be asked or what's needed. The book is a mixture of our and other people's experiences, but takes readers on a journey of everything they're likely to go through when facing the end of their lives, plus how exploring our mortality can mean that we can live better lives. It's definitely a book for everyone – everyone should read it at some point.

Q **Where did the name for your progessive funeral service Poetic Endings come from?**

A I made up the name – it just came into my head one day. It came from my love of poetry and it's to do with how poems don't necessarily talk about beautiful things, they cover some really difficult subjects, but the whole point of a poem is that they take something difficult and package it in this beautiful way – like I wanted to do with funerals. Funerals are not always beautiful with a happy ending for someone who has just died peacefully in their sleep. They're often really tragic and difficult. But we can bring some poetry to them, not in the form of words, but in the form of how we handle the situation and our approach to it. I think we all deserve a poetic ending. Ultimately it will help the people who survive us to live their best lives.

Q What do you believe makes a good farewell?

A Emotional engagement, taking a risk, getting involved in aspects of the funeral that seem scary. Transformation happens when people are prepared to take a risk and do something that's out of their comfort zone, whether that's standing up at the funeral and saying something, or seeing the person who has died. What we're trying to do as funeral directors is help people to get in touch with what it is that would be a risk for them and help them feel safe and supported in doing it.

Q Could you share some of the most memorable services you've been involved with organising?

A I think they're all really memorable in their own way. Sometimes they're really complex – we've built yurts in the middle of the countryside and we've had sound systems for people who really loved music and the quality of sound was super-important to them. Equally we've done really simple things where it's been 20 minutes, early in the morning, at the crematorium chapel, one person sitting inside, a bird singing outside, and just supporting that person saying their goodbye. Often, the most simple funerals are the most difficult, the most emotionally complex. Funerals are varied – I can talk about all the different coffins and hearses you can have, but really it's the emotional engagement with the process that makes a funeral unique and memorable.

Q Are there any trends occurring in the funeral industry right now?

A Not really trends, but we've noticed the level of engagement increasing. Rather than just going along with what a funeral director on the high street says, people are wanting to get involved and ask lots of questions and participate. Almost every call we get now is from someone who's very engaged, has a whole list of questions for us and is consulting different funeral directors to find the right one for them. That's something we weren't experiencing a few years ago. It's becoming much more mainstream, because different generations have different expectations.

Q Do you see any common misconceptions among your clientele about what kind of funerals you can and can't have?

A Yes, that a person has to be embalmed before you can see them, or that funerals have to take place in a church. That you have to have a vicar, or that you can only have five seconds of music. People often have very restricted ideas about what funerals are, and they're often very surprised when they find out that there are actually very few rules. In general, people can have the service they want – we start with a blank page and create the rituals and ceremonies that serve the people who attend the funeral.

Q Do you have any favourite resources about death and funerals?

A Amy Cunningham in New York – she's one of my favourite funeral directors.

"Victorian funerals are a bit of a myth perpetuated by the funeral industry"

"I personally embrace
for my death. Firstly,
told my kids what I
I want my ashes to g
that I want played at
there's relief in that
I know that they're p

planning
if I've already
want, where
o, the music
the funeral,
because
repared"

TV personality Jeff Brazier, in an interview for Lost for Words, Royal London's 2020 exhibition in collaboration with RANKIN

Interview with
Ben Buddy Slack
Founder of The Swan Song Project

The Yorkshire-based singer-songwriter reflects on the power of music to help individuals prepare for the end of their lives

Ben Buddy Slack realised the importance of saying goodbye after his grandmother died. Based in Yorkshire, the folk musician now runs The Swan Song Project, which pairs a professional songwriter with anyone facing the end of their life and terminal illness. Together, they write and record a song as a fitting tribute to that person's legacy.

Q **What inspired The Swan Song Project?**

A It was when I lost my grandma. She always loved music and we'd sing and play music at her house. Towards the end of her life she was in a care home. My uncle and I went to visit her one day when she was pretty unresponsive, until we started playing "Black Velvet Band", which was her favourite song. We were holding her hand and she started tapping her fingers and her face kind of lit up – it was a really powerful moment and memory. A few years later, my mum and great-auntie were speaking about it and I thought, "Wouldn't it have been nice if we had recorded Grandma singing with us?" Then I thought, what if my grandma had written a song – how nice would it be to have a song she'd written for us? At the time I was doing a lot of songwriting with people in the community, working in prisons and various settings, and I wondered if I could do that with people at the end of their lives. I contacted a few hospices in Leeds and Bradford and they all got back to me and said yes! We started by working with [the charity] Marie Curie.

Q **Tell us a bit about the kind of songs you write with people facing the end of their life. What kind of topics come up?**

A We've written songs about all sorts of things. Many choose to express their love to their friends and family. A lot will reflect on their life, sometimes reaching new conclusions about it. There's one song I remember from fairly early on in the project. The woman came to us feeling quite angry – she'd had a really hard life and, just when things were looking up, she got cancer. She felt like she'd had a really hard time. So we thought her song would probably be about that. But then, when we started talking about it, she thought she'd been really lucky in some ways as well. She felt lucky to have her children and felt proud of them. By the end, the song was no longer an angry song – there was a bit in it about hard times, but the overall message was that her life had been a good one. Sometimes the songwriting process can help to change people's perceptions. When you start thinking about your life and putting it into an art form, you might see it in a different way. It's such a privilege to have those conversations with people.

Q **As a songwriter and musician, what does it mean to you to use music in this way? Has it changed how you feel about music?**

A I went into it a bit knuckleheaded. I thought, "Oh, I'll be fine," but it's like dealing with compounded grief, which is tough. I don't think there's a way of doing it properly without making a connection with someone. So when you lose them, it hurts. One thing I've learnt is that it doesn't matter how much you rationalise or intellectualise death. I know from the beginning that the person I'm working with is at the end of their life, but you can't think your way out of the feeling that comes with that. I don't know if that's changed the way I feel about music but I would say it's deepened it. I'm a big believer in music and songs – they're incredibly powerful. Seeing that in practice, I've thought more about how songs work and the life of a song. They don't have to be for mass consumption. If a song is made just for one person and it means a lot to that person, then that's all it needs to do. Someone might only want their wife to hear it, and that's completely fine.

Q Why do you think songwriting is a good form for saying goodbye?

A I guess a song feels communal. You can sit and listen to a song together. A song washes over you in a certain way, along with the beauty of the music and the voices. I remember hearing about people who would ring someone's answerphone over and over again after they'd gone, just to hear their voice. Voices are important. Like with my grandma – it would have been so easy to press record, but we never thought to do it. There's something about the structuring of a song that consolidates ideas, too. Writing a song can help you say what you really mean.

Q What kind of impact has working on The Swan Song Project had on your feelings about your own mortality?

A Well, when you're young, you don't want to think about this stuff. I've written songs with a few young people. I worked with a woman who was the same age as me and that was particularly tough. It makes you aware that there's no logic or justice to it. You can get a terminal illness at any age. It's definitely changed my view of my own mortality in that sense and given me a bit more appreciation for my health – it's pushed me to do some things I was putting off. I'm quite lucky as my partner works at one of the hospices and we talk about it openly. But then I speak to other people and I realise they aren't comfortable talking about it. Part of our aim with the project is to try to improve the conversation about dying. We started a podcast during lockdown that talks about the songwriting craft and music that means something to those with bereavement. Sometimes hearing a song is easier than reading about it.

Q What are your hopes and ambitions for The Swan Song Project?

A My big goal is to make swan songs part of our culture. That when someone is getting older or facing the end of their life, it's normal for them to think, "I'm going to write my song." That would be a beautiful thing. You don't have to do it with us, or with a professional musician. I hate music snobbery and how we think musicians are different to the rest of us. They are just people who practise music – everyone has music taste and a way of expressing themselves that's unique to them. Anyone can write a song. It can just be a little tap and it doesn't have to be pitch perfect. One of the things that keeps me going with the project is when people tell me, "Oh, I wish this had been around a year ago when my dad was still here." That's why I'm looking forward to writing more and more songs.

"My big goal is to make swan songs part of our culture. That when someone is getting older or facing the end of their life, it's normal for them to think, 'I'm going to write my song'"

*TV presenter Konnie Huq,
from an interview as part
of Lost for Words, Royal
London's 2020 exhibition in
collaboration with RANKIN*

*"I've never really cons
will. Or I think [dyir
young. The loss of my
to write my will or g
I think it might have
with at the time. On
it spurred my husba
and, actually, I think
I probably was back*

dered writing my own

g is] far away, I'm so

parents didn't spur me on

t my affairs in order, but

been too much to deal

 with COVID-19 has

d on to write a will

I'm in a better place than

then to do it anyway"

Interview with
Barry O'Dwyer
CEO of Royal London

Insurance expert and leader of the Royal London group on why talking about death is so important and the warming traditions of the Irish wake

As CEO of the mutual life, pensions and investment company Royal London, Barry O'Dwyer knows a thing or two about death. The Irishman is passionate about demystifying financial matters and has seen first-hand how preparing your paperwork appropriately for your death is a sign of love. He oversees Royal London's campaigns and political lobbying, which aim to make an impact on issues such as probate mismanagement and funeral poverty.

Q **Why is talking about and planning for death important?**

A It's a strange subject to be so taboo, because it's a natural part of life. Thinking about death triggers an insight into grief for many people, and it's understandable why many of us are reluctant to go there. I don't like thinking about the death of anyone close to me. The subject has to be handled and discussed sensitively with loved ones. So why do I think talking about death is so important? Obviously, in my line of work I see the positive impact of making financial plans – receiving a life insurance payout, for instance, or the proceeds of a funeral plan, can be the difference between a whole family coping financially or struggling financially. Making these sorts of plans, ultimately, is a form of love. It may not be the most romantic purchase you'll make but it might be one of the most loving. That's one of the key reasons I think talking about death is so important.

Q **What does "dying well" mean to you?**

A Being content that you've led a good life and you've made a positive impact on your family and the community that you leave behind, making sure that you don't die with regrets about not having told people you love them. These are the sorts of things that come to mind first and foremost when I think about dying well.

In a practical sense, there's something about having made plans so that your loved ones know what you wanted – talking to them in advance, leaving them with the information they need, making sure that you pass on as much wealth as possible to the people or causes you loved, which is a big part of what we do as an industry. In general, lots of people are unprepared for their death. Accepting death while you're alive means you can make the most of the time that you have. It's this idea that you feel you've had a positive impact on people when you're alive and you're leaving them with good memories.

Q **Any top tips or simple tricks for leaving behind more wealth?**

A The core thing to do is to write a will, so that you're deciding where your money goes. Lots of people die without one. People have this perception that if you die without a will it's not a big problem because your wealth will automatically go to your loved ones, but it may not. Essentially, if you die without a will, the law will determine where your money goes, and it may not be in the direction that you'd expected.

The other thing is there are lots of practical ways in which people can limit the amount of inheritance tax they pay. Obviously, it applies at higher levels of wealth and it's perfectly right and appropriate to pay inheritance tax, but there are ways in which you can make sure that you don't pay too much, meaning you can leave as much as possible to your loved ones. That's where good financial planning comes into its own and this is where financial advisers can add a huge amount of value, helping you to understand the best way of structuring your finances before you die.

Q **Has working in this industry changed your own relationship with dying?**

A It's hard to know because I'm struggling to think about how I perceived it before! I'm an actuary, and part of your training to become one is to understand the financial consequences associated with the different ways people die, and conversely, the financial consequences of people living much longer than they expected. That inevitably makes you think differently. When I hear a phrase on the news like "thousands of lives could have been saved", I automatically think of it as "thousands of lives could have been prolonged". They can't be saved. The way we talk is an example of the way we fail to acknowledge death as an inevitable. But we're all going to die. One of the stats that blows my mind is how about 50% of new mortgage applicants don't take out life insurance. I'd like to speak to each one of them and remind them that they're not in full control of when they're going to die, but they can be in full control of what the aftermath looks like for their families. If mortgage applicants are in their thirties or forties, they're probably not going to die for the next 20 to 25 years, but if they do, the consequences for their families could be horrendous. So maybe it's changed my relationship with death because, like a lot of people in this industry, I've become passionate. I'm passionate that people should understand how to protect their families.

Q **This book touches on different cultural attitudes to death in the UK. You're Irish, how do you see these differences?**

A My view is, fundamentally, people aren't all that different in the world, but customs and beliefs are. It's quite interesting that they can make a real difference to the experience of death. The most obvious difference for me is religious belief. I've seen people take huge comfort in their religion at a time of death. Particularly when it's an untimely death. The thought that it isn't final provides huge solace for some people. More generally, though, I grew up in this environment of open caskets and wakes, so that if you attended a funeral, you could see the person one last time. Often, people would touch or kiss the corpse. Some of these traditions probably seem odd, but they do serve a purpose in helping communities to heal and honour their dead.

The concept of the Irish wake is possibly a more extreme version of what I've seen more and more in modern funerals in the UK. There's a move away from that slightly austere, traditional set-up, and more recognition that a funeral should be a celebration of a person's life. It's a chance for those left behind to remember the person that they've loved. I think it's becoming more common to share funny stories involving the person concerned at their funeral. That helps the people who are left behind, and it's nice for everyone to think their friends and family might be laughing at their funeral and it hasn't been a totally depressing affair. Some of the traditions of the Irish wake are reflected in the fact that people are more accepting that a funeral should be a combination of sadness and celebration. It can be an occasion to laugh together while remembering the person who has gone.

Q **Are there any quotes, books, films or poems about death that are particularly meaningful to you?**

A I like this quote, from Mark Twain – "The fear of death follows from the fear of life. A man who lives fully is prepared to die at any time." That reminds me of what I was saying about preparing and actually it being a very loving thing to do, to prepare for the eventuality. A film that sticks in my mind is *Coco*, the Pixar film. It's a really nice way of introducing the subject to kids and it's a great film for families to use to talk about death.

"I grew up in this environment of open caskets and wakes, so that if you attended a funeral, you could see the person one last time"

Further resources

Here are some easily accessible resources and websites that can point you in the right direction when it comes to tackling the logistics of wills, tax, probate, legacies and more in the UK and Ireland

Useful charities and organisations

Age UK
The UK's leading charity for supporting older people.
ageuk.org.uk

Alone
An Irish charity supporting older people to continue living independently.
alone.ie

Citizens Advice
Provides information on the legal rights of residents in each nation of the UK.
citizensadvice.org.uk

Citizens Information
Current, comprehensive information on social and public services in Ireland.
citizensinformation.ie

Compassion in Dying
Offers guidance on end-of-life planning, supporting people to make advance decisions, also known as living wills.
compassionindying.org.uk

Dying Matters
Run by a national coalition of individuals and organisations, this campaign aims to raise awareness and build an open culture of talking about dying, death and bereavement.
dyingmatters.org

End of Life Care Coalition
A group of charities and organisations calling for high-quality and personalised care as people approach the end of their lives.
endoflifecampaign.org

HMRC
The UK government's department for guidelines and information on tax, including inheritance tax.
gov.uk/government/organisations/hm-revenue-customs

Revenue
Ireland's government site for tax and customs, with information on gift and inheritance tax.
revenue.ie

First steps

A list of useful links to helpful charities and organisations to help you think about, plan and record your end-of-life wishes, as well as deal with the paperwork after a loved one dies. The range of topics they cover includes money, support and legal issues.

Age UK: legal information
Information on a variety of legal issues, such as choosing a power of attorney and making a will.
ageuk.org.uk/information-advice/money-legal/legal-issues

Citizens Information
Essential information on what do when someone dies in Ireland and voluntary services that offer support.
citizensinformation.ie/en/death/when_someone_dies_in_ireland.html

Royal London
A document that simplifies recording all your funeral wishes and personal and financial details so that you have them in one place.
royallondon.com/articles-guides/learn/bereavement/planning-ahead-to-protect-your-family/when-im-gone-list

A guide to where to find help when someone dies. It covers everything from how to deal with debt, resources for financial aid for paying for funerals and the support that's available for bereaved children.
royallondon.com/articles-guides/your-money/when-someone-dies

The Irish Hospice Foundation
Resources to help with planning for death and end-of-life care.
hospicefoundation.ie/programmes/public-awareness/think-ahead

The Money Advice Service
Information on how to deal with money after a death, including paying for funeral costs and sorting out an estate when there's no will.
moneyadviceservice.org.uk/en/categories/when-someone-dies

Power of attorney

Information on how to give a trusted loved one power over your legal decisions, should you become incapacitated through ill health.

General guidance
royallondon.com/articles-guides/ your-money/power-of-attorney

Nation-specific guidance

England and Wales
gov.uk/power-of-attorney

Scotland
mygov.scot/power-of-attorney

Northern Ireland
nidirect.gov.uk/articles/managing-your- affairs-and-enduring-power-attorney

The Republic of Ireland
citizensinformation.ie/en/death/before_ a_death/power_of_attorney.html

Your legacy

If you're looking to use your last wishes to create some positive changes when you're gone, here's some further information on how you can donate your organs, tissues and body, leave money to a charity in your will, or set up a charitable trust.

Organ donation in the UK
In England, Scotland and Wales your organs will be automatically donated after you die, unless you opt out. In Northern Ireland you must opt in if you'd like to donate your organs.
organdonation.nhs.uk

Organ donation in the Republic of Ireland
In Ireland you need to register yourself as an organ donor.
hse.ie/eng/about/who/acute-hospitals-division/organ-donation- transplant-ireland

Donating your body in the UK
Information about donating your body to medical research in the UK.
hta.gov.uk/faqs/body-donation

Donating your body in Ireland
In Ireland, you can register to donate your body for scientific research at a number of further-education institutes, such as:

The Royal College of Surgeons in Ireland
rcsi.com/dublin/about/faculty-of-medicine-and-health- sciences/academic-departments/anatomy-and-regenerative- medicine/anatomical-gift-programme

Trinity College Dublin
tcd.ie/medicine/anatomy/donation

UCD School of Medicine & Medical Science
www.ucd.ie/medicine/bodydonation

Leaving money to a charity
Information on how to make a financial gift to a charity in your will.
rememberacharity.org.uk/leaving-a-gift/how- to-leave-a-gift-in-your-will

Setting up a charitable trust
Guidance on setting up a charity in the UK.
gov.uk/set-up-a-charity

Writing a will

In order to ensure that your end-of-life wishes are going to be met, it's important to write a will. The links below cover the specifics of drafting a legally binding will in the UK and Ireland, whether you need a solicitor and where to find one if you do.

General guidance
royallondon.com/articles-guides/your-money/making-a-will

Nation-specific guidance

England and Wales
gov.uk/make-will/writing-your-will

Scotland
lawscot.org.uk/for-the-public/what-a-solicitor-can-do-for-you/making-a-will

Northern Ireland
nidirect.gov.uk/articles/making-will

The Republic of Ireland
citizensinformation.ie/en/death/before_a_death/making_a_will.html

Do you need a solicitor?
citizensadvice.org.uk/family/death-and-wills/wills/#h-whether-you-should-use-a-solicitor

Finding a solicitor

England and Wales
solicitors.lawsociety.org.uk

Scotland
lawscot.org.uk

Northern Ireland
lawsoc-ni.org/solicitors

The Republic of Ireland
lawsociety.ie/Find-a-Solicitor

Applying for probate

Guidance on the process of applying for the legal right to handle someone's estate after their death.

Nation-specific guidance

England and Wales
gov.uk/applying-for-probate

Scotland, where it's referred to as "confirmation"
mygov.scot/confirmation

Northern Ireland
nidirect.gov.uk/articles/applying-probate

The Republic of Ireland
citizensinformation.ie/en/death/the_deceaseds_estate/dealing_with_the_deceaseds_estate.html#l56c52

Inheritance tax

Trying to wrap your head around the different thresholds and exemptions? Here's the government guidance on inheritance tax in the UK and Ireland, as well as some explanatory reading.

Government outlines

The UK
gov.uk/inheritance-tax

The Republic of Ireland
revenue.ie/en/gains-gifts-and-inheritance/gift-and-inheritance-tax-cat/index.aspx

Help with inheritance tax
moneyadviceservice.org.uk/en/articles/a-guide-to-inheritance-tax

ageuk.org.uk/information-advice/money-legal/income-tax/inheritance-tax

You

fun

Section Two

The dead are everything and nothing like us
Kevin Toolis

Many cultures around the world spend intimate time with the bodies of the deceased, which brings comfort to the bereaved. Here, the Irish writer tackles the UK's modern-day alienation from corpses and explores the importance of acknowledging the body that once was

You never forget your first corpse.

For a start, they are awful quiet.

They don't talk, say a word, or react to anything you say to them – how you've always hated their guts. Or love them so much that your heart is breaking. You can shake them, beat your fists upon their chest, call them a bastard, take them in your arms for a heart-comforting embrace, kiss their lips, and still the dead do nothing. They just lie there, immune from the world and its myriad responsibilities.

Do you remember that game you played as a child? Pretending?

Pretending to be dead.

Stilling your breathing, eyes closed, not moving a muscle. Or waiting for the little flicker of the eye, heave of the chest, that gave the game away. Gotcha!

Pretending is a game the dead are truly hopeless at. No "real" person could ever mimic their stolid silence, their immovable virtue.

And here's another existential epiphany: the dead don't look well.

Even as your eye flicks across this page, your heart is pumping blood around your arteries at roughly 2lb per square inch of pressure. Live humans are meaty, inflated balloons of blood, muscle, sinews, nerves and fat.

But cut the pump and the whole thing deflates to the floor like a rubber sack. The blood drains from cheeks, your fingers, your arms, and pools in the lower limbs or your back.

Faces sag, muscles cleave flaccid and sallow skin shrinks on ivory finger bone. You look pale, wizened, dead in fact.

Corpses are cold, too.

Every human being that you have ever touched before, in love or anger, was a warm-blooded mammal. But the dead are so cold – stone-on-an-outside-path-in-winter cold – that it is almost impossible to believe that this thing, this imperfect facsimile of a being you have known, could ever have been human.

Except the dead were, and are, human. Those two impossible things, at the same time too.

Still human. A dead one of Us. The locus of our grief and anguish for all that is lost. The physical body of our beloved dead.

For millennia we have struggled to articulate the difference with talk of "souls" and "spirits", to explain the very difference after breath stops and the great animating current of consciousness, personality, has been sucked out, leaving behind just dry, ice-cold remains.

This visible deadness, this contradictory moment of encounter between the Living Us and the Dead Them, is the very epicentre of all human civilisation. Spawning an eternal search for eternal life and numerous priesthoods, religions, temples, gods, persecutions, wars and countless millions of other deaths of heretics and non-believers who fail to believe in our particular promise of a deathless heaven.

And that's just the corpse.

But the biggest difference about meeting your first corpse has got nothing to do with whoever is inside the coffin-shaped box. Mother, child, man or boy.

The real insight breaks out inside you.

Once you've got over the idea that you've not stumbled onto the set of some trick-camera series, it slowly begins to dawn that today's show is not even a show. Or a special occasion at all.

That the dead person is no one special. And has not even been on TV. That they are just another ordinary mortal. Like you.

A slow, deflating, dawning realisation.

The nub of it all.

Here at last, voluntarily or otherwise, you are now playing your own, full part in a non-game of certain extinction, where, one by one, all the players lose their lives, generally unnoticed and not cared about by a wider world.

Mortal Reality. With its own, certain rules.

We lie all the time in the rest of our daily lives.
Often for good reasons.

"I love you."

"This weekend, sure. I'll be there."

"I'll stop drinking from now on. Never again."

"Your arse does not look big in... "

We cheat the truth. Make up stories. Go back on
ourselves. Reverse. Say we are sorry. Kiss and make
better. And live to lie another day.

But death is a script that can't, and will not, be reversed
by anger, tears, cardiopulmonary resuscitation, money,
status or appeals to some Higher Power. Or further
promises.

Nothing on Earth can ever make this dead thing sit up,
cough and begin again.

Every Could-Have-Been has hardened into a Never-
Was. Every word of their story is now a past tense –
the right, the wrong, where they lived, loved, who
they were, how they got sick and died. Heroic or Stoic
or Afraid. As we might be.

It's all Final. Forever. Finished.

Dead.

The end point where all our stories stop and our
own true mortal powerlessness is inescapable.

There, now within the grasp of your own warm mortal
flesh, is the objective defiance of Every-Possibility-to-
Be. A dead human. So ordinary, and yet the very mirror
of your own Death-to-Come.

**Kevin Toolis is a Bafta-winning writer and the author
of *My Father's Wake: How the Irish Teach Us to Live, Love
and Die.* His new book, *Nine Rules to Conquer Death,*
is published by Oneworld.**

"For millennia we have struggled to articulate the difference with talk of 'souls' and 'spirits', to explain the very difference after breath stops and the great animating current of consciousness, personality, has been sucked out"

Your funeral checklist

Over the course of your lifetime, you've probably spent hours, if not days and weeks, planning your wedding(s), birthday parties and holidays, yet probably have rarely taken a minute to think about your funeral. While the idea of planning your own might seem unappealing and make you feel uncomfortable, it's an important step in ensuring your final wishes are met and, as we've said before, it will save your loved ones having to make arrangements while they're grieving. This checklist highlights some of the key considerations when it comes to prepping your send-off.

Funding

You can't take it with you, right? As part of the division of your assets, it's important to leave a sum behind to cover the costs of your funeral arrangements, if you can afford to, that is. This will save your family members having to suddenly find a sizeable chunk of money to pay for it. Whether it's through savings, an insurance policy or a pre-pay funeral plan, there are many options for covering the cost of your own funeral in advance. If you have life insurance it's worth checking the details of your policy. To help cover funeral costs, many providers will make an initial payment before a life insurance plan is paid out in full. If you're not in a position to save money and you pass away without any assets to your name or family members able to cover the cost, a public health funeral can be arranged. Local authorities are obliged to pay for a dignified funeral for those without the means to pay for one and will cover the costs of a coffin, funeral director and burial or cremation.

The announcement

How would you like the world to find out about your passing? Some people still choose to make an announcement in the local newspaper, whereas others prefer to post on social media now. Perhaps you would rather keep the news more private and just share the information between family and friends.

Funeral directors

You probably wouldn't buy the first pair of shoes you saw in a shop window, and deciding on a funeral director is no different. Shopping around is essential, both for securing the best deal and to ensure you find someone that you're confident understands your needs. A good funeral director will listen carefully to your wishes and do their utmost to make them happen.

Cremation or burial?

One of the first decisions to make about your death is actually quite simple – burial or cremation? It's best to read up on both options and their economic, environmental and spiritual implications before making a choice. Whether you opt for a burial or cremation, you need to think about your final destination. Would you like your ashes scattered in a favourite spot or carried with family members when they visit other countries so that you can continue your travels after death? If it's a burial you're going for, is there a spot in a family crypt with your name on it or would you prefer to have a natural burial in the woods? The choice can be yours!

Graveyard garments

"I wouldn't be seen dead in that!" – or so we say. If it's important to you that you wear something you're comfortable being seen dead in, it may be worth picking out your outfit in advance and letting your loved ones know your wishes. You might also want to think about what you would like other people to wear to your funeral and plan a dress code. Would you prefer them to attend in traditional black attire or would you rather they're decked out in your favourite colour – or even the full colour spectrum of the rainbow? Alternatively, you could ask people to wear something that's meaningful to you, like the shirt of your beloved football team, or to dress up as characters from your favourite film. Feel free to get creative!

Flowers

Do you love roses and carnations like Paris Hilton, or loathe hydrangeas, as Madonna does? If so, it might be wise to consider which kind of floral arrangements you want to accompany your coffin at the funeral. Perhaps you don't want flowers at all and would rather people make a donation to a charity of your choice. Make sure to put that in writing.

The service

Are you going for a religious or non-religious funeral, elaborate or eco-friendly, something celebratory or sombre and low-key? You might want to prepare a playlist of your favourite songs for the service or decide on particular poems you wish to be read. Perhaps there's a singer, musician or contemporary dancer among your circle of friends or family who you can ask to do a short song or performance. Whatever you do, don't feel pressured by tradition when making your funeral arrangements – it's all in your hands.

The wake

After the party it's time for the after-party, of course. While funerals are always emotional affairs, the wake often helps to lighten the mood and allows your nearest and dearest to celebrate your life, share stories about you and support each other. Create a guest list, decide on the budget, refreshments and location – perhaps your favourite restaurant or a family member's home. Making these decisions in advance will help you create a wake that reflects who you were as a person, as well as lifting the burden of responsibilities from your loved ones.

What are my choices?

"To accept death is to accept that this body belongs to the world. This body is subject to all the forces in the world. This body can be broken. This body will run down"
Sallie Tisdale, *Advice for Future Corpses (And Those Who Love Them): A Practical Perspective on Death and Dying*

In our everyday conversations, it's often considered taboo, too morbid or just a bit awkward to talk about funerals. We therefore avoid making a clear plan or putting our wishes down on paper, and this, sadly, can create a burden for those who live after you're gone. They're already having to deal with pain, emotions and endless phone calls, so why not save them the guesswork (and potential arguments) about what kind of funeral you'd like and choose a plan of action yourself?

Burial or cremation? Lilies or carnations? Debussy or Dua Lipa? Do you want to donate your body to science? There's a wealth of resources out there that can help you decide – not to mention people whose job it is to sort it all out. Making arrangements for your future funeral and, if you can, sharing the details with your nearest and dearest beforehand can save a lot of trouble – both emotionally and financially.

When it comes to making these decisions, it's important to remember that so much of what we expect to happen at funerals isn't mandatory but, rather, has come about due to traditions passed down through generations. For example, did you know that, while it's a legal necessity to have a body cremated or buried, the rest of the ceremony is completely up to you? You don't have to hire a hearse, a limousine or any other specialist vehicle to transport the coffin. Maybe you want a pink Hummer to be your last ride. You're not legally obliged to have a coffin either, and there are plenty of good-looking and sustainable alternatives these days (further details on page 80). Embalming is not obligatory and, some would argue, not necessary – it's worth doing some research to find out what you think. When it comes to the ceremony itself, you have the option of holding it at home or any other venue personal to you, rather than an official or religious one.

Choosing a funeral director is often a task left to grieving family or friends, but there's no reason why you can't research one for yourself, particularly now that there's a wide and growing variety of funeral services to meet all kinds of wishes. There's also the option of skipping the undertaker completely – there's no law that requires you to have one, although there is an advantage to having a professional on board to take care of some of the trickier bits of funeral organising, such as storage and transportation of the body. Many of the death specialists we interviewed in the making of this book also agreed that everyone should be aware of their rights in their search for a funeral director. It may sound strange to refer to them as "consumer rights" but that's essentially what they are, and there are plenty of resources to help you navigate the process, particularly if you're struggling with the cost, as we outline on page 86.

Basically, don't feel pressured into having to settle for the first funeral director you find or the one that's closest to where you live. Like many things in life, it's important to shop around – Judith Moran, of Quaker Social Action, which aims to relieve funeral poverty through its initiative Down to Earth, compares this to looking for the right washing machine on page 141 – so make sure to choose the service that's most compatible with your vision and budget. Again, if you have the opportunity in advance, it's worth doing. "Pre-booking" a funeral may sound ridiculous, but that's only because we're used to avoiding the subject. Even a list of two or three options will help your next of kin – it's much better for them to be confident they're making the right choice than searching through brochures or websites while grieving.

Another of the main arguments for planning your own funeral ahead of time is the need to manage its cost. During a time of bereavement, people are often forced to make hasty decisions when they're at their most vulnerable, and expenses can rack up quickly. Grieving relatives might also feel under pressure to upgrade your funeral arrangements because they don't want to appear mean. If you're choosing a natural burial site, picking a spot next to a tree will mean you don't have to pay for a headstone or other marker. If you're having flowers, requesting that they're sourced from the gardens of family and friends will do away with the expense of formal floral arrangements, which also produce non-compostable waste. You can ask your friends to pitch in with the catering, too. People often find it a relief to provide practical support at a time when it's hard not to speak in platitudes – and helping in this way also means they won't have to face a buffet of sausage rolls (unless that's one of your last wishes).

Cultural differences

Ready to embark on a journey of deciding what kind of funeral best represents you as a person? Whether you're religious or not, why not familiarise yourself with some of the funerary traditions that have been knocking around for millennia? Of course, each religion and faith carries specific traditions and rituals for death and burial, which have contributed to the options available for funerals. And while representing all religions of our multi-faith society would be impossible, here's a brief overview of the traditions favoured by different religions and cultures that could potentially inspire your final choices.

Baptist

Led by the local pastor or minister, funerals usually take place in a church or crematorium following a mourning process that includes a viewing service. This offers family and friends the opportunity to say one last goodbye.

Buddhism

Following in the footsteps of the Buddha, cremation is the most popular choice for Buddhists. However, the number of those going for natural burials is on the increase, which isn't surprising, given that they're an environmentally friendly alternative that's very in tune with the religion's concept of *samsāra*, or rebirth.

Catholicism

In Catholic tradition, a prayer vigil is organised on the eve of the funeral as a send-off for the departed, usually at the church where the service will be held. When it comes to the funeral itself, the proceedings follow the format of a Requiem Mass and include Catholic funeral hymns or sacred music.

Church of England

In terms of location, a Church of England funeral can take place almost anywhere, from a church or crematorium to a natural burial site. They're also pretty open to non-churchgoers, too – you don't have to be a member of the Church of England to have one. Hymns such as "Amazing Grace" and "The Lord's My Shepherd" are popular in church settings, but having music is a choice.

Eastern Orthodox Church

Wakes, usually one-day long, are held before the funeral in Orthodox tradition. During the funeral itself, an offering of koliva – a dish made from boiled wheat and honey or sugar – is placed near the head of the coffin to represent death and resurrection. Cremation is completely forbidden.

Hinduism

According to Hindu customs, the body of the person remains in a coffin at their home after their death until the cremation. During this period, flowers are placed at the feet of the deceased and a garland of flowers or a necklace of wooden beads arranged around their neck. For men, a paste of sandalwood or ash may be smeared on their forehead, while women have turmeric on theirs. And then there's the dress code – white is a must, black is a no-no.

Humanism

For those who feel like having their life celebrated without the presence of a religion, a humanist funeral service could be the perfect option. Borrowing the structure from traditional funerals but focusing on the individual and their personal stories, humanists use a format that's tailored to each person's wishes.

Judaism

Jewish funeral traditions are rich and vary according to the denomination. However, the presence of a guardian – called a *shomer* if male, *shomeret* if female – who's responsible for tending to the body from the moment of death until the burial, is common. Another ritual sees mourners ripping off pieces of material from their own clothes as a demonstration of their grief, and wearing the torn garments for a week after the person has died.

Islam

Funeral preparations are traditionally separated into two sections – Ghusl and Kafan. As part of the former, the body of the person who's died is washed multiple times by family members of the same sex. Following that, the Kafan includes the body being wrapped in layers of large sheets.

Religious Society of Friends (Quakers)

Quakers emphasise simplicity and silence in their funeral services. Anyone can speak if they choose and the ceremony is led by an elder or a minister, known as a Friend. The service typically takes place at a meeting house and ends with all the guests shaking hands.

Sikhism

A cremation is the traditional preference for a Sikh funeral, although burials are permitted if a cremation isn't possible. The ashes are typically scattered over water; headstones and plaques aren't used. As with many other major religions, funerals should be arranged as quickly as possible, usually within three days.

Spiritualism

Because of its openness to different cultures, spiritualism often allows for funerals to be organised for people who were never active members of the religious community but shared their beliefs. Spiritualists are open to both cremation and burials, as well as green funerals.

Burial at sea

While not technically a culture or religion, sea life is indeed a lifestyle. And with it comes the choice of departing this world through one last encounter with the big blue. Sea burials are often considered expensive and complicated, but the UK actually has three locations where they can be arranged: off the Needles, at the westernmost tip of the Isle of Wight; at a spot off the south coast between Hastings and Newhaven in East Sussex; and off Tynemouth in North Tyneside. In Ireland, government guidelines recommend scattering ashes at sea, but if a sea burial is wanted, it must take place at least 50 miles from the shoreline and follow official regulations.

How do other countries deal with death?

Different societies have their own mourning methods, which are passed from generation to generation. According to academics, culturally defined death rites are a means of countering the transience of life with the longevity of tradition. While we're likely familiar with how our own community mourns, it's interesting to examine how others around the world deal with death, as this ultimately gives us alternative perspectives of both death and life.

1

Mexico celebrates Día de Muertos on the first two days of November, coinciding with All Saints' Day and All Souls' Day. During this national holiday, which dates back to Aztec festivals, family and friends build private altars in the cemeteries of their loved ones, bringing with them the deceased's favourite foods, as well as items that belonged to them in life. This is believed to encourage the souls of the dead to be more attentive to the prayers of the living.

2

Influenced by the melting pot of West African, French and African-American cultures in the region, jazz funerals have become tradition in New Orleans. Dating back to the late 1800s, funeral processions are led by a brass band that, after initially playing sorrowful dirges, switches to upbeat tunes once the dead have been buried.

3

While Denmark is traditionally Protestant, Danes still observe some non-Christian and pagan superstitions surrounding death. For example, when someone is expected to pass away, it's common to leave a window open to give their soul a chance to escape. This is also a way for loved ones to cope with their grief, as they may find solace from the fresh air.

4

In Ghana, coffins are increasingly seen as a way to reflect individuals' passions in life. This has led to the popularisation of "fantasy coffins" in the shape of objects ranging from cars to Bibles and even fish.

5

In Turkey, funerals are only one aspect of commemoration. *Mevlit* ceremonies are also traditionally held to honour the deceased's memory and to provide a support network for loved ones who have been left behind. These usually happen on the 40th and 52nd day after the death, as well as on its first anniversary, with family and friends gathering in a circle to share food and drink and read passages from the Qur'an, narrating the life and death of the Prophet Muhammad.

6

According to Vajrayana Buddhism, typically followed in Tibet and Mongolia, after death, the body becomes an empty vessel while the soul moves on. In order to return the body to the Earth, it is chopped into pieces and exposed to the elements and carrion birds at the top of a mountain. Known as sky burials, these have been practised for thousands of years and continue to be popular.

7

Due to dwindling space for cemetery plots, South Korea passed a law in 2000 that requires graves to be removed after 60 years. While cremation has increased in popularity as a result, some families opt to have their loved ones' remains compressed into gem-like beads that are then displayed in their home.

8

In the Tana Toraja regency of Indonesia, death is not approached as a final, severing event. Instead, the bodies of the deceased are preserved and cared for in the family home in the weeks, months and even years following their passing.

9

Every five to seven years, the Malagasy people of Madagascar participate in *famadihana*, or "the turning of the bones". Families exhume the bodies of their dead in a celebration at the ancestral crypt, complete with a band and dancing, as a way of passing on family news to the dead and commemorating their loved ones.

Considering cremation

"Elaborate burial customs are a sure sign of decadence"
J.G. Ballard, *The Complete Short Stories*

While it's very much a conventional choice today, cremation hasn't always been part of funeral traditions. Looking back through history, there's evidence of Ancient Greeks and Romans practising it. But in the early 5th century, with the growing presence of early Christianity, whose followers disliked cremation, the practice disappeared. It wasn't really considered again until almost 1,500 years later, when Sir Henry Thompson, surgeon to Queen Victoria, brought the conversation into the mainstream by writing a paper and campaigning in support of cremation. Ever since, it's been a subject of much debate.

Over the past century, the popularity of cremation has been steadily growing – from being part of 15% of all funerals in the 1950s, it now occurs in more than 75% of them, according to The Cremation Society. It's often seen as a budget-friendly alternative to traditional burials and a response to the lack of space in cemeteries. However, its negative environmental impacts have increasingly become a point of discussion in recent years. While it does decrease the amount of space a body takes up, a single cremation uses almost as much energy in the form of electricity and gas as a car trip from London to Zurich, and releases 400kg of carbon dioxide into the atmosphere.

Another recent trend is direct cremation. Perhaps you're not into the idea of a ceremony, or simply can't afford one. Direct cremation occurs without a ceremony or the presence of anyone, and is often billed as the cheapest option by funeral services. However, it's important to remember that while it might be presented as such, it certainly doesn't fit the needs of every family and there may be other affordable options for you to explore.

And then there's the big question of what to do with the ashes. Even if you decide to remain in an urn, there are so many styles to choose from – do you go for plain, opulently decorated or something made from upcycled woven textiles? The niche brand Funeria makes urns look so high end you'll practically be housed in a piece of contemporary art. In case you're feeling more adventurous and wish to live it up one last time, you might want your ashes to be turned into a diamond, launched into space or scattered from a hot-air balloon.

David Bowie's unexpected impact on the death industry
When David Bowie passed away in 2016, tributes poured in from the many fans who were touched by his music. But his legacy goes beyond the art he left behind: he also sparked a trend for the no-frills funeral. After the musician opted to be secretly cremated, the low-cost funeral service Simplicity reported a 400% increase in demand for direct cremations.

Eco-friendly funerals

"Not only is natural burial by far the most ecologically sound way to perish, it doubles down on the fear of fragmentation and loss of control. Making the choice to be naturally buried says, 'Not only am I aware that I'm a helpless, fragmented mass of organic matter, I celebrate it. Vive la decay!'"
American mortician, author and blogger Caitlin Doughty, *Smoke Gets in Your Eyes – and Other Lessons from the Crematorium*

So, you've stopped buying single-use plastic and have finally incorporated composting into your daily routine; you've swapped your old petrol car for an electric, and decided to shop local instead of at one of the big-name supermarkets. But how do you apply that green mindset to your funeral? Being conscious of the environment is now an important mission of the death industry, and going green isn't as difficult or costly as you may think.

One of the main tasks in organising a funeral that's not going to hurt the planet you're leaving is minimising the carbon footprint of your farewell. It means saying no to embalming, a process that includes swapping the blood with usually highly toxic chemicals in order to preserve your stunning looks. The growing natural death movement also encourages burials in a coffin made from eco-friendly materials, such as bamboo or banana leaf, at a shallower depth. This not only enables the body to decompose faster but also reduces the release of methane, a greenhouse gas produced by deep burials. The movement's proponents also advocate choosing a natural burial site as your final resting place – *naturaldeath.org.uk* has a useful list of locations in the UK and Ireland.

However, be warned: funerals aren't immune to the phenomenon of greenwashing that's emerged as a commercial response to the climate crisis. It's important to research the services you're using to ensure the impact is as positive as it seems.

While an eco-friendly funeral might sound a bit of an extreme choice at first, remember that you don't have to be vegan, an environmental activist or member of the Green Party in order to throw yourself one. Eliminating some of the traditional notions – such as the need to have a massive mahogany coffin, elaborate floral wreaths and a fleet of black cars – doesn't have to clash with elements of a traditional funeral. You can still incorporate family customs and religious traditions, as well as your favourite Celine Dion power ballad, into the service without causing any negative consequences for the natural surroundings you're about to become a part of.

"Being conscious of the environment is now an important mission of the death industry, and going green isn't as difficult or costly as you may think"

Choosing a coffin

"Choosing the right final resting place is a good thing to tick off your funeral to-do list"

"Dying is a troublesome business: there is pain to be suffered, and it wrings one's heart; but death is a splendid thing — a warfare accomplished, a beginning all over again, a triumph. You can always see that in their faces"
George Bernard Shaw, playwright

Now's the time to get creative. Just like picking a bed will set the tone for a new bedroom (Scandinavian pine or velvet upholstery?), choosing the right final resting place is a good thing to tick off your funeral to-do list. Your future mourners might face pressure to guess what you would have wanted, or even feel influenced by the possibility of the shame and stigma unfairly associated with picking the cheapest option. They might end up spending more than they can afford, even though you don't give two hoots about having an expensive send-off.

Before you decide, you might want to know that there's no law that obliges a person to be buried or cremated in a coffin. The only requirement is to have the body covered and out of view from a public highway in order to respect public decency. This means, once again, that there are many choices.

But let's start with the most traditional options. Coffins today don't just come in wood and metal. In an attempt to create more environmentally friendly choices, there's been a surge in the availability of coffins made in alternative materials that are more biodegradable — including seagrass, wool and bamboo.

One of the pioneers of the eco-friendly coffin revolution is the Kent-based company Ecoffins, whose options include banana leaf, pine and cardboard. In fact, cardboard is another popular choice that not only has a minimal impact on the environment, but is also a blank canvas of sorts, offering the opportunity for the family or the person themselves to decorate it as they wish. It's about time we got rid of the connotations of cardboard being part of a "pauper's funeral", which is an old-fashioned term anyway.

Shrouds are a simple and somewhat elegant option, and an inexpensive one at that: prices start at about £195, or around €220 (though you can choose to spend more on a bespoke embroidered version). A hybrid of eco-friendly coffins and shrouds, soft coffins are a signature of Devon business Bellacouche. They're made from recycled and natural absorbent materials that are hidden inside a felt-encased wooden base, which comes with a detachable cover that's placed over the shroud.

And for those with a penchant for interiors, you may want to take inspiration from the Shelves for Life concept debuted by designer William Warren at the 2005 London Design Festival — a beautiful bookcase you can use during your life that can then be transformed into a coffin once you're gone.

What would you find in an ancient Egyptian tomb?
The ancient Egyptians had many different practices when it came to burials. For example, the deceased would have most of their organs removed and placed in canopic jars, the lids of which would depict ancient gods who they believed would protect the body parts. The brain was extracted through the nose and discarded, as it was thought to be unimportant. The heart was left intact inside the body, as it was believed that its weight signified how much good an individual had done in their lifetime, which would be measured in the afterlife.

The ultimate outfit

If you had to wear one look for the rest of eternity, what would it be? Mourning dress became de rigueur (aka commercialised) during the Victorian era, when specialised shops selling fashionable widow's weeds (black clothing worn by widows) and accessories expanded their business into burial gowns. These gowns were designed in pastel shades of shiny satin and crepe, with details including ruches, false shirt fronts, lace, ribbons and bows. Nowadays, they're made as unisex garments, offering the idea of a unified and forgiving outfit that will put the focus on the person rather than what they were wearing.

Remember, good funeral planning means the event will be as meaningful to your guests as you would want it to be. In more recent times, there's been a shift towards expressing the person's individuality through their funeral dress. A hand-knitted jumper? Your favourite silk dressing gown? Your prized Liverpool FC shirt from the year they won the Champions League? However, if you're planning to be cremated, you won't be permitted to include any leather or rubber pieces — including biker's regalia and footwear with leather or rubber soles. Glasses, too, can't be cremated, due to their negative environmental impact. In case you're an avid naturist, you shouldn't feel the need to choose an outfit at all. It's possible to attend your own funeral nude, although a body must be shielded from public view with some kind of a covering.

Washing and dressing someone who's died can be an important part of the mourning ritual, depending on your faith. Before Muslim funerals, the closest family members of the person who's died are responsible for shrouding them in layers of simple white cloth.

In the Jewish tradition, too, bodies are dressed in a simple linen or muslin shroud, with yarmulkes (skullcaps) and prayer shawls also included for men.

But what's an outfit without the right accessories? There are numerous stories of what certain celebrities have taken into their coffins with them. Allegedly, the writer Roald Dahl was buried with, among other things, a few chocolates in his pocket, while Andy Warhol is said to have been clutching a bottle of his favourite Estée Lauder fragrance as he was lowered into his grave. Or maybe you're about the simple pleasures, like Bob Marley, who was reportedly sent off with his red Gibson guitar, a Bible and some greenery. Notes, letters, precious jewels, toys or photographs — your options are pretty open when it comes to picking what you're going to take with you, but do consider the environment if you can.

Underground fashion

Visual artist, designer and researcher Jae Rhim Lee is bringing sustainable fashion to the death industry with her biodegradable burial suits, which are embedded with mushroom spores that break down the body into clean compost that's full of nutrients. The new strain of fungus she's developed, named the infinity mushroom, destroys harmful chemicals that the body releases as it decomposes.

Famous last words

"*The best eulogies are said to be a balance between sincerity, nostalgia and lightness of touch — but, honestly, it's the meaning that counts, not the performance*"

A memorable eulogy

John Steinbeck's landmark novel *The Grapes of Wrath*, published in 1939, features a particularly memorable eulogy. Against the backdrop of the Great Depression, the Joad family embark on a trek from Oklahoma to California in search of work. When Grampa Joad dies en route, former preacher Jim Casy is asked to make a speech over his grave. He says: "This here ol' man jus' lived a life an' just died out of it. I don't know whether he was good or bad, but that don't matter much. He was alive, an' that's what matters."

Just like with any other piece of writing, the key to a good eulogy is solid structure that will support the ideas and stories you want to tell. There are plenty of online resources that retell the experiences of people who went through the effort of writing their own eulogy. An interesting piece of advice that experts like to give is that you should work backwards — starting with the emotion or reaction you want to achieve, and then finding the right words to express it.

The best eulogies are said to be a balance between sincerity, nostalgia and lightness of touch — but, honestly, it's the meaning that counts, not the performance. Including poems in a eulogy is a common practice, and can help those who aren't able to find their inner wordsmith. In addition to the rich heritage of traditional remembrance poems that have been passed on for generations, there's an arsenal of funeral classics written by some of the greatest poets in modern literature. "Funeral Blues" by W.H. Auden, "Because I Could Not Stop for Death" by Emily Dickinson and "When Great Trees Fall" by Maya Angelou are a few popular choices.

And if all else fails to inspire, it might be the perfect moment to revert to music. In a 2019 survey, Frank Sinatra's track "My Way" was voted the number one funeral song, with Andrea Bocelli and Sarah Brightman's "Time to Say Goodbye" coming second and Eva Cassidy's evergreen "Over the Rainbow" in third place. Don't let these dictate your choice, though — creating the ultimate soundtrack to your farewell can be a very healing process. Some humorous choices could be considered — think Mariah Carey's "Obsessed" or "When the Party's Over" by Billie Eilish.

Funeral poverty

"While the cost of funerals has grown in the past 10 years, the average income has not. You don't need amazing mathematical skills to see there's a discrepancy in this equation"

Just like with any other life event, funerals can end up being a very costly affair. Rarely discussed, but very much present in our society today, funeral poverty affects more people than you might think.

What is funeral poverty?

According to the Royal London *National Funeral Cost Index 2020*, the average cost of a funeral in the UK is about £3,800 (the price of an average used car). Meanwhile, a basic Irish funeral can cost anywhere between €2,950 and €7,500, and burial plots can range from €1,400 to €9,000, according to Royal London research carried out in 2018. In short – it's a lot of money to leave behind. With the cost of death being so significant, the inability to cover one's funeral fees is causing financial difficulties for many who are left behind. To put it simply, funeral poverty is the shortfall faced by those who are unable to pay for a funeral – and research shows that 9% of people face a shortfall of almost £2,000.

How does it happen?

While the cost of funerals has grown in the past 10 years, the average income has not. You don't need amazing mathematical skills to see there's a discrepancy in this equation. Research carried out by Royal London in 2020 found that 9% of people took on debt arranging a funeral. Out of those, 21% were forced to borrow from family and friends and 8% chose a cheaper funeral. This can happen for a plethora of reasons. For example, a loved one's living costs incurred later in life might have exceeded what they managed to save, leaving you to cover some or all of their funeral payments. You might also be a young person with little in the way of savings who suddenly loses their parents and is faced with the awful responsibility of covering funeral costs despite not having a fund dedicated to this sort of event. Or you might want to fulfil your grandmother's wishes for repatriation – the practice of sending the body or ashes to one's country of origin – but have no real way to afford such an expense.

There can also be hidden costs in the process of planning a funeral. Lack of price transparency is a significant issue in the funeral industry. While organisations such as Down to Earth – an initiative run by the charity Quaker Social Action that offers support and guidance for those affected by funeral poverty – are lobbying to change that (see details of its Fair Funerals pledge on page 142), there's still a lot of work to be done. If you're arranging a funeral and are concerned about costs, you can ask funeral directors to talk you through their low-cost options.

If I'm broke, will I have to have a pauper's funeral?

When we think of a "pauper's funeral", we think of dark, Dickensian times and a lot of social stigma. But things have changed since then – organised by your local council, public health funerals are an option for those with little or no financial backing, as well as those with no traceable family. It's a basic funeral organised with monetary aid from the local authority, supported by public funds. It's also fairly common – a Royal London report says the total spend on public health funerals in the UK in 2018/19 was £6.3 million.

Is there help available?

Yes. If you're on a low income and receive certain benefits you may be able to get a Funeral Payment (or Funeral Support Payment in Scotland) from the government to help you pay for a funeral you're arranging – see page 102 for more information. Organisations such as Quaker Social Action and the Muslim Burial Fund are also here to provide you and your loved ones with financial support, as well as the information needed to help support you if you're facing funeral poverty. Their work on good practice in the funeral industry through lobbying the government and publicly discussing these issues means we can feel optimistic about change. But as with any problems in life (or death), it's essential to reach out to those who are here to help you. This isn't just your issue – it's the issue of many.

Funerals in the UK and Ireland: facts and figures

The ceremonies after death have developed substantially over the centuries, with various rituals and traditions coming in and out of fashion. While the traditions differ among religious groups, as well as the non-religious, what happens in the end is about following the family's wishes – there's no one-size-fits-all approach.

33,000
years old – the earliest-known burial site in Britain

£3,290
is the average cost of cremation in the UK

£4,383
is the average cost of burial in the UK

22.7%
of the Irish population opt for cremation

140,000
people choose burial each year in the UK

Cremations are more popular than burials, with only a third of the UK's population opting for the latter. This could be due to the fact that they tend to be more expensive than cremation: in 2020, the average cremation funeral cost £3,290 versus £4,383 for a burial (figures taken from Royal London's *National Funeral Cost Index*).

Despite burials being less popular than cremation, 140,000 people in the UK choose the former each year. In Ireland, however, burials are still the top choice: as of 2019, only 22.7% of the population opted for a cremation, according to The Cremation Society.

While organ donation is seen as a positive deed in Judaism, autopsies are frowned upon as they're seen as sacrilege of the body. The faith will allow them to happen if it's required legally or if carrying out an autopsy will help to save the life of another person, but a rabbi must be in the room when the procedure is happening.

In Hinduism, it's normal for the family of the deceased to wash the body, although ghee, honey, milk and yogurt are typically used to cleanse the departed, rather than water.

Cremations in Ireland can be traced back to the Stone Age, when ashes were placed in stone structures; after the emergence of specific pagan beliefs, they were placed in decorative urns. It wasn't until the introduction of Christianity to the country, around the beginning of the 5th century, that burial became the norm.

Researchers at Cardiff University and the Natural History Museum have found that Iron Age Britons used to dig up the deceased to allow communities to interact with them. There's no concrete evidence of why this happened, but it may have been considered a way for families to help their relatives on their way to the afterlife.

Muslim graves should be perpendicular to the direction of Mecca, the Islamic holy site. The deceased are usually wrapped in a white cloth and placed on their right side, facing Mecca.

The oldest-known evidence of a burial in Britain was found in south Wales in 1823 during an archaeological dig. Located in a cave, the remains were originally thought to have been those of a Roman woman; scientific advancements have since revealed them to be of a young man, possibly a tribal chief, who was likely ceremonially buried more than 33,000 years ago.

The cost for a burial is highest in London. Highgate Cemetery, in north London, where Karl Marx and Malcolm McLaren's final resting places can be found, is the country's most expensive. In 2017, it cost £16,475 to have the right to a grave here, but machine digging added £1,850 to that.

There are some faiths where burial is the only option. In Islam, and most forms of Judaism, cremation is totally prohibited.

Space is a big issue with regard to burials. In the UK, it's estimated that half the cemeteries will be full within the next seven years. Gardens of Peace, the largest dedicated Muslim cemetery in the country, opened its first site in east London in 2002, with 10,000 graves; by 2018, all of them were occupied. According to the UN, today, there are 7.8 billion of us on Earth, but by the end of the century it's thought there will be 10.9 billion, which means that we may soon need to look for alternative solutions to the traditional ground burial.

There's an alternative to burial that's becoming increasingly popular: alkaline hydrolysis, which involves dissolving bodies in an alkaline solution. It's more colloquially known as "green cremation" and already available in some states in the US and provinces of Canada.

In parts of Ireland, it's still common practice for the body of the deceased to be displayed in the family home prior to the funeral so that people can come to pay their respects. In the past, wakes started with the female neighbours of the departed washing the body to prepare it for being laid out on a kitchen table or bed.

Design your funeral

What kind of funeral would you like? Your final send-off doesn't have to be dry; it can be an expression of your individuality, the after-party of a life well lived and a comfort to those you leave behind. Take a moment to jot down your wishes, from your favourite songs, to what you might like to wear in the coffin and your final resting place.

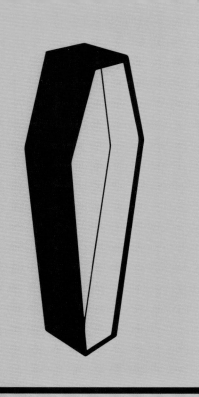

1. Draw your future coffin

2. A vision board for your funeral after-party

Interview with
Ahmed Alsisi
Chaplain and founder
of White Rose Funerals

Having spent the past decade
supporting the Muslim community
in south Wales, the funeral director
discusses the Islamic outlook on
death, funerals and grief

White Rose Funerals is Wales' first Muslim funeral directors. Established in 2010 by Ahmed Alsisi and his brothers, the family-run business has grown over the past decade to serve all faiths as well as the non-religious – something that Alsisi admits was "a very tough barrier to break".

Q Let's start at the beginning – why did you set up White Rose Funerals?

A It's been quite a journey, to be honest with you. It all started when I was told at a gathering that there was a lack of services within Cardiff and south Wales that cater for faith-based funerals for Muslim, Hindu or Jewish communities. Initially I just wanted to do Muslim funerals – I knew more about them, being a Muslim myself. Since the Cardiff and south Wales Muslim community is small, we all know one another, so it was easy for me to provide this personal service.

Q White Rose Funerals was the first Muslim funeral service in Wales, which must have come with its own set of challenges. What were some of the difficulties you faced?

A Wales needs to catch up with laws and regulations to help families with faith have a dignified send-off for their loved ones. To begin with, there were a lot of problems – issues with same-day burials, weekend services and registration, the coroner and a lack of education around faith-based funerals. There were a lot of things to tackle at one time and, being so young and inexperienced, I had to do a lot of research and reading and make contacts.

Q As you mention, same-day burial is a common aspect of Islamic funerals. What are some other unifying elements?

A The Muslim community, and also the Jewish community, don't like the idea of an invasive post-mortem. Another thing we all agree on as Muslims is, no matter what, no cremation. That's a big no-no. The idea of cremation seems too harsh for members of the Islamic faith because, for our whole lives, we've tried to avoid burning in fire. At Western and Indigenous funerals, it's more a celebration of life, whereas in Muslim communities, it's about the family – them having lost someone special and making sure they're OK. To give them time to mourn, the whole community cooks for them and makes sure they have enough food.

Q More generally, how would you describe the Muslim outlook on death?

A Our faith tells us to live your life to the fullest, to enjoy life, to marry, to eat, to go out, to travel, to receive the best education, but to never forget that, at any moment, you can leave this world. Our approach to death is that it's not the end, it's part of a new life, and we have this understanding from a young age. We accept the idea of death and dying, and I'd like to say we're more positive because we believe we'll be reunited [with loved ones who have died]. I've lost my grandparents and I miss them like crazy, but I'm at peace because I know I will meet them again and I just have to be patient until that time.

Q Alongside providing Muslim funerals, you now serve individuals of all faiths and none. What prompted this shift?

A A few years into doing Muslim funerals I was approached by families of different faiths, asking me to do funerals for them. I thought this might be a good way to show integration in a new form, because funerals are a very sensitive time in our lives, and you need people you can totally trust to perform such a service. We pride ourselves on being the first Muslim funeral directors in Wales, but we're also the first Muslim funeral directors to cater for all faiths and no faiths. I don't think anyone else in the UK does this, just because it's a very tough barrier to break.

Q What's been your secret to breaking down that barrier?

A What makes us different [from other funeral arrangers] is the fact that my family and I see our job as starting at the funeral rather than ending at the funeral. We keep in touch with almost all our families for years just to make sure they're OK and aren't struggling.

Q Finally, what impact has your choice of career had on your personal view of death?

A It's only reaffirmed what my parents taught me as a child – that I should utilise my time wisely before I die. When I pass, I want to look around and say I've done my best for myself and everyone around me. I can have fun, but I've learnt that it's not all about having fun. Now my way of "having fun" is making sure that I'm healthy and happy, that my parents and children have food on the table, that my wife is content, that my brothers and sisters are looked after and that my community is safe.

"I have already in what I want to be I just want someo in a forest and th need a marker or

my head decided
done [when I die].
ne to dig a hole
row me in. I don't
anything else"

Actress and drag queen Divina De Campo, from an interview as part of Lost for Words, Royal London's 2020 exhibition in collaboration with RANKIN

Interview with
Charlie Phillips
Photographer

The Jamaica-born image-maker speaks about his career capturing the funerals of west London's Afro-Caribbean community

The British photographer Charlie Phillips, born in Jamaica in 1944, has been documenting London's Black community for more than half a century. Known for his photographs of the people and places of Notting Hill and its surrounding areas, he's captured both daily life and important moments in the history of this part of the city, from race riots and protests to the early expressions of the famous carnival.

After Charlie's aunt passed away in 1963, he started documenting the funerals of west London's Afro-Caribbean community, taking photos of services in cemeteries such as Kensal Green. Images from his extensive visual archive of the ever-changing funeral process of his community formed the 2014 photography book *How Great Thou Art: Fifty Years of Afro-Caribbean Funerals*, and his work has featured in exhibitions at Tate Britain and the Museum of London and is included in the Victoria and Albert Museum's collection.

Q What drew you to the idea of documenting Caribbean funerals in London?

A I was taking pictures of everything. I thought I was going to be here for five years and was hoping that, when I went back to Jamaica, I could show them what life was like in England. So, funerals were among the documentary [work] I was doing. I was documenting our lives in the 1960s, and funerals are a part of life. The first funeral I photographed was my Auntie Suzie's, in 1963.

Q How did people react when you were taking pictures?

A At the time they all thought I was crazy, but no one took notice of it. I had grown up in the community, people knew me and, over the years, people got used to me. I was the only one documenting, I'm the only insider who documented our story and our history. We're coming up to the seventh generation [in the UK] and there's been a gap in our history and that's why I've documented it.

Q How would you describe a Caribbean send-off?

A Death in our community is a celebration of someone's life, so this is why they party after. If you had a good funeral, it was an event, you didn't have to be invited, you could just go. This was for our generation but now the youngers today tend to invite select people. Before, it was open to everybody and anyone could come and pay respect to the dead. It was to celebrate the person's life — after all the mourning and all the crying everybody goes and has a party. And you can see in my photographs, it's like a discotheque, a big celebration.

Q What are some of the Caribbean funerary traditions that have been brought over by the community and continued in London?

A The dress code, the celebration, the hymns. "How Great Thou Art" was the main hymn. In the early days we used to have a very strict dress code to wear black and lilac, they were the main colours of funerals. Everyone also has to wear a symbol that represents the person, so if the lady's favourite colour is red, you have to wear some red. I remember there was a lady who was a dressmaker and she loved her machine, so she had a wreath that looked like a Singer sewing machine and it went in her grave. Another tradition is that if a guy likes his drink, when his coffin is going down you pour some whisky — it's like, "Have a drink on me." Or if someone likes cigarettes, you could throw them in. We also have volunteers to fill the

"It's not about just taking you and putting you in a box, it's about celebrating"

grave up, we do the whole thing. And then the women will come in and decorate the grave. The guests participate in the funeral and burial as part of the tradition. After the service, a group of people will stand by the grave and continue singing. It's not about just taking you and putting you in a box, it's about celebrating.

Q What are some of the most important rituals within a funeral?

A The dressing of the body. It's when the family comes round to put on the favourite suit or dress of the dead person. That's a specialty in our community — you don't really see that too much any more.

Q You've spent so many years documenting other people's funerals. Has that made you reflect on what you'd like for your own?

A It's kind of spooky for me now, I'm getting on and I don't know when my time will come. I've made some plans for what I want. We have to meet our makers. [There will be] no crying over me, and I'd love to be buried at sea, but that's not going to happen. I don't think the younger generation really think about [their funerals] these days, but the older generations made plans way in advance — they would leave money to one side. My aunt left money on the side for her burial, and she knew how she wanted to dress and what music she wanted.

Q Will you continue shooting funerals?

A No, but I have this archive that documents how much funerals have changed over the years. We can look back and see how it was. It's good because it makes people look and think about funerals in a different way. It's not just about putting them in the ground and covering them over and having a little cry. It's making people aware that they can be spiritual and [a funeral can be] uplifting.

Malin Andersson, the Love Island star and model, from an interview as part of Lost for Words, Royal London's 2020 exhibition in collaboration with RANKIN

"When I was younger at sc spoke about death. No one you on death. I think, as b feel awkward about the co of death because we don't happen and we don't know or respond to it"

ool, no one
educated
umans, we
versation
vant it to
ow to act

Further resources

Planning your own funeral in advance is becoming more common, but it can still be challenging to know where to begin. Here is a list of charities, organisations and resources that can help you explore what options are out there when it comes to funeral planning and decide what's right for you

Funeral planning

The ins and outs of funeral planning can be tricky to get your head around, and you may not know where to start. The following resources offer some straightforward guidance on what arrangements need to be considered when it comes to thinking about your funeral.

Citizens Advice
Guidance on arranging a funeral in the UK.
citizensadvice.org.uk/family/death-and-wills/funeral-services/arranging-a-funeral

Citizens Information
A guide to arranging a funeral in Ireland.
citizensinformation.ie/en/death/after_a_death/funerals.html

Funeral Choice
A website offering price comparisons for funeral directors across the UK, with more than 3,000 listed.
yourfuneralchoice.com

Funeral directors – professional associations
Select a funeral director who's a member of a professional association, as they have codes of practice and a robust complaints procedure.

The UK
The National Association of Funeral Directors (NAFD).
nafd.org.uk

The Society of Allied and Independent Funeral Directors (SAIF).
saif.org.uk

The Republic of Ireland
The Irish Association of Funeral Directors.
iafd.ie

Non-religious funerals

Humanist Association of Ireland
Information about humanist funerals and a contact page for celebrants in your area.
humanism.ie/ceremonies-2/funerals

Humanist Society Scotland
Provides information about humanist funeral services and a list of registered celebrants.
humanism.scot/humanist-ceremonies/funerals

Humanists UK
Advice on humanist funerals and memorial ceremonies.
humanism.org.uk/ceremonies/non-religious-funerals

The Institute of Civil Funerals
An institute that offers a database of funeral celebrants available to lead non-religious funeral services.
iocf.org.uk

Religious funerals

Jewish Joint Burial Society
Founded in 1969, this UK society plans Jewish funerals, covering 17,000 community members across 39 synagogues.
jjbs.org.uk

Muslims Funeral Services
A charity offering guidance on planning a funeral in line with Islamic teachings.
mfs.org.uk/Bereavement_Guide_for_Muslims.pdf

The Art of Dying Well: A Guide to Catholic Funerals
A simple guide to Catholic funerals and cremations, including music, funeral proceedings and frequently asked questions.
artofdyingwell.org/what-is-dying-well/catholic-funerals-cremations/guide-catholic-funerals

The Buddhist Society
A guide to planning a Buddhist funeral in the UK, as well as works on death and dying.
thebuddhistsociety.org/page/buddhist-funerals

The Church of England
Funeral information and guidance from the Church of England, including on arranging or attending a funeral and planning ahead for your own.
churchofengland.org/life-events/funerals

The United Synagogue
The largest synagogue movement in Europe, this network offers information and guidance on organising a burial for Jewish people.
theus.org.uk/arrangingaburial

Help and support with funeral costs

With the average cost of funerals rising all the time, many people in the UK and Ireland regularly struggle to pay for them. However, there are a number of ways you can reduce the expense, as well as charities that offer financial support to families so they can meet these costs.

Child Funeral Charity

A charity offering guidance and financial support for parents in England and Wales who are arranging a funeral for their baby or a child aged under 16.
childfuneralcharity.org.uk

Down to Earth

An initiative by Quaker Social Action that supports people affected by funeral poverty.
quakersocialaction.org.uk/we-can-help/helping-funerals/down-earth

Muslim Burial Fund

The Muslim Burial Fund offers support and guidance to Muslims who need help to fund the costs of a traditional Muslim burial.
muslimburialfund.co.uk

The Children's Funeral Fund for England

A government fund for parents who've lost their baby or child under 18. The Children's Funeral Fund is available to all parents, regardless of income.
gov.uk/child-funeral-costs

Government support for funeral payments

The UK

These government guidelines give a clear idea of the support you can expect to receive from it in covering funeral costs and advise how to access these funds.
gov.uk/funeral-payments

The Republic of Ireland

Ireland also has funding in place to help cover the cost of funerals if you or your family are unable to pay. This link has information on how to access it.
citizensinformation.ie/en/social_welfare/social_welfare_payments/death_related_benefits/benefits_and_entitlements_following_a_death.html

Further information

National Funeral Cost Index Report

Over the past seven years, Royal London has produced an annual report on the costs of funerals in the UK and Ireland.
royallondon.com/media/research/national-funeral-cost-index-report-2020

Paying for a funeral

Royal London offers tips on how to pay for a funeral and suggestions for how to keep costs down.
royallondon.com/articles-guides/learn/bereavement/what-to-do-when-someone-dies/paying-for-a-funeral

The Fair Funerals pledge

This initiative addresses the issues surrounding funeral poverty, encouraging funeral directors to commit to being open about their most affordable prices to avoid people feeling obliged to pay beyond their means.
fairfuneralscampaign.org.uk/content/about-us

Burials at sea

The UK
There are quite specific procedures for funerals at sea. The UK government website provides a breakdown of how you can access a licence in order to have sea burial.
gov.uk/guidance/how-to-get-a-licence-for-a-burial-at-sea-in-england

The Republic of Ireland
This government website offers a set of voluntary guidelines for those in Ireland considering burial at sea.
gov.ie/en/service/de81b8-burial-at-sea

Green funerals

For those who are conscious of their carbon footprint, green funerals are becoming increasingly popular. Below are links to organsiations that provide information on how to organise an eco-friendly funeral.

Green funeral directors
The Association of Green Funeral Directors (AGFD) can connect you with funeral homes that focus on more sustainable and eco-friendly options.
greenfd.org.uk

The Natural Death Centre
A charity that provides information on all aspects of dying, from handling bereavement to consumer rights. It also has details of a plethora of resources dedicated to natural and eco funerals.
naturaldeath.org.uk

Funeral guidance for the LGBTQIA+ community

A list of resources with specific information on funerals for people within the LGBTQIA+ community.

NHS Guide to LGBTQIA+ funerals
The NHS has created a guide with vital information on how to handle the death of someone within the LGBTQIA+ community, which includes considerations of how to plan a funeral when your family doesn't know that you're part of the queer community.
www.sad.scot.nhs.uk/bereavement/supporting-lgbtplus-people-around-bereavement

Queer Funeral Guide
Funeral professional and trans activist Ash Hayhurst has created an extensive guide to organising a funeral for a member of the LGBTQIA+ community.
goodfuneralguide.co.uk/wp-content/uploads/2019/09/Standard-PDF-queer-funeral-guide.pdf

Funeral planning from prison

Whether you're in prison yourself or have family members who are incarcerated, you may have questions about how to organise or attend a funeral. The below links give guidance on how to make this happen and what to consider.

Day release to attend a funeral
Information on the process to apply for day release to attend a funeral in the UK.
insidetime.org/leave-to-visit-dying-relatives-or-attend-a-funeral

What happens when you die in prison?
If you expect that your life may come to an end while you're in prison, the funeral process is quite different. This information sheet guides you through funeral planning if this is the scenario you are facing.
death.io/happens-die-prison

Say

Section Three

goo

ing

dbye

That ~~difficult~~ tender conversation
Dr Kathryn Mannix

Drawing on three decades
of experience with patients
at the end of their lives,
palliative care pioneer
Dr Kathryn Mannix explores
how to discuss the topic
of death with a loved one

"My mum has cancer and she's not getting better. How can I find out what care she wants as her health gets worse?"

I've become an agony aunt for conversations about death: messages come from dying people who can't get their loved ones to listen, from adults wondering how to broach the conversation with their elderly or sick relatives, and from parents asking how to explain the death of a cherished person to children. All are perplexed about how to approach it. All fear doing harm.

How can we talk about dying?

Let's start by relaxing. Talking about death won't make anybody die sooner. It's safe to talk. Even if it feels sad to discuss these things, having important conversations now can reduce the level of distress that can often come later.

It's helpful to think about this conversation as a process that is progressing a little at a time, rather than a bang-boom-done event. We don't have to talk about everything all at once. We simply need to open up the possibility of talking. Conversation flows better if it's by mutual agreement, so why not invite each other to the conversation?

"Mum, I've been thinking a lot about what might happen if you get sick in the future and the doctors ask me about how you want to be looked after. Do you think we could chat about that some time?"

"Kids, I've had a great life but I'm old and I won't live forever. I want to talk to you all about how I'd like to be looked after at the end of my life. Can we arrange to talk?"

"Pals, you know my illness is getting worse and I'm worrying about my family. I'd like to talk to you about supporting us as I'm dying, and you keeping up your support for them afterwards. Could we mull it over?"

What do we need to talk about?

Start with what feels easier or more pressing. Many people feel more comfortable talking about events after their death than talking about dying itself. They may have opinions about their funeral – the venue and music – while others' attitudes may be more "do what you like, I won't be there". Some people have a specific personal or practical concern they want to settle before they are too unwell to sort it out.

Once you've broken the ice, the follow-up conversations won't feel as awkward. It's good to plan something happy and distracting to talk about afterwards, too. Be creative!

There are practicalities, such as where to live during the last part of life. At home? With a relative? In a care home? A district nurse can provide useful insights into what extra care can be provided at home and where the local care homes are.

Details matter. Things such as preferences for company, music, pets, TV, fresh air, privacy, quiet. People can be surprised by our choices, so don't expect them to guess. FYI, I'd like the window open and quiet talk radio – if you're cold, put a jumper on.

There might be legacy conversations, with the subjects ranging from writing out recipes or recording an interview that hands down family stories, to writing a will or having the pleasure of gifting things while you're still alive.

Just as important as the practicalities, though, are the "heartfelt conversations". People want to say thank you to each other, to put old disagreements aside, to forgive and be forgiven. People want to express their love – our gift to them is to listen. Don't let embarrassment shut these tender conversations down. They are words from someone's heart, and giving people time and attention allows them to reach peace of mind.

Above all, let's discuss what matters most dearly to us. Let's help the people looking after us to prioritise our values.

What is dying like?

I've described this to thousands of people over my medical career. Its simplicity has often surprised them: they were expecting pain or horror. In fact, it's usually gentle. Provided the symptoms of the illness we are dying from are well controlled, it's not an uncomfortable process.

We become gradually more weary. We sleep more. Sleep gives us an energy top-up, but not for very long. In our final days we become unconscious. That's not like sleep — we don't notice as we lose consciousness. Initially, we dip in and out of consciousness, and we may wake up enough to chat from time to time.

Eventually, dying people are unconscious all the time. Their bodily organs are slowly shutting down. Their breathing begins to change, with cycles of fast-to-slow and deep-to-shallow respirations, sometimes quiet and sometimes noisy, all completely automatic and not caused by or causing distress.

Finally, usually during a period of slow breathing, there's a breath that just isn't followed by another one. No panic, pain or palaver. Sometimes it's so gentle the family doesn't notice for a while.

Knowing about this process helps everyone to be a little less anxious beforehand, and to recognise the stages of the process as it progresses. Knowing what to expect helps families to be assured that children won't see anything frightening if they visit; recognising the stages helps to gather the right people at the right time. Being aware of what to expect can help those tender conversations about what matters most, where we would like to be looked after, whose companionship we would like.

Remember to live

Dying people are simply living close to the end of their lives. They don't need us to have solemn faces or use special voices. They appreciate the normal things: contact, news, laughter, a cuppa. There's a freedom in knowing what's important, and dying people have usually worked out what that is. It's not money or stuff or status. It's people, relationships and love. Have the conversation. Unless you're immortal, of course.

"Above all, let's discuss what matters most dearly to us. Let's help the people looking after us to prioritise our values"

End-of-life discussions:
your checklist
Dr Kathryn Mannix

Since you've probably never died before, it can be hard to plan for. This list is a combination of things that families and individuals have found useful in end-of-life discussions, and things I've seen bring great consolation to people. It's not exhaustive, so please do add your own items. Good luck!

Funerals

What are the individual's preferences about burial or cremation, church or secular ceremony, music, readings, eulogy, celebrant, final resting place of body or ashes? Should the dress code be mourning or party colours? Should there be flowers or a collection for a good cause? Family only or open invitation? Which type of coffin should it be, what clothes should be worn in it, should any memorabilia be put in it? Is it possible to pay in advance? How much can you pre-plan things? Did you know that funeral directors, celebrants and clergy will all make home visits if you'd like to plan ahead?

Wills

If you don't make a will, the law decides who inherits everything you leave behind and that may not be the people you would have chosen. Even if you own very little and have no savings, it's easy and wise to make a will, and ensures the right people inherit the things you'd like them to have. Even better, give gifts to them in person before you die!

Place of care

Do you want to live at home? With a relative or friend? Is that practical? Think about the ease of getting a cup of tea, getting to the toilet, managing steps and stairs. Would you consider extra help at home? Or moving to somewhere that provides care? Perhaps it's worth checking out local care homes – their attitudes, their atmosphere, their charges.

What matters most to you?

Is it a place? People? A pet? A way of life? A spiritual practice? This is worth thinking about and telling your supporters. In the future, if you're too unwell to decide things, they can help to ensure the decision makers take your values into account.

Achieving a balance between comfort and treatment

Most of us prefer to be comfortable, but some medications used to manage pain or breathlessness occasionally cause drowsiness. Being drowsy may be acceptable or it may be something you really don't want. Where would you draw the line? Would you accept some drowsiness in order to be comfortable? Or would you prefer to accept some discomfort in order to be alert?

Finding the balance between quality of life and length of life

As our health deteriorates, previously helpful treatments that have side effects or require time in hospital may offer less chance of recovery. It's worth thinking about whether you want to live as long as possible, no matter how taxing the medical treatments to preserve your life may be, or whether you want to live as comfortably as possible, even if that means not living quite so long. Examples of this decision include whether or not you would accept a ventilator and admission to an intensive care unit; a treatment/operation that carries a significant risk of increased disability afterwards; or hospital treatment for an infection that is getting worse at home.

Decision makers/attorneys

Unless you take the correct legal steps, no one else can speak for you if you become temporarily or permanently unable to speak for yourself. You can appoint one, or several people, to be your attorney(s) and this gives them the legal power to decide about treatments and other care for you – but only if you can't do that for yourself. There's more information online for those living in the UK and Ireland:

England and Wales
gov.uk/power-of-attorney

Scotland
publicguardian-scotland.gov.uk/power-of-attorney

Northern Ireland
nidirect.gov.uk/articles/managing-your-affairs-and-enduring-power-attorney

The Republic of Ireland
citizensinformation.ie/en/death/before_a_death/power_of_attorney.html

Are there any medical treatments you want to avoid?
You can make an advance decision to refuse treatment (sometimes called a living will), which will protect you from unwanted medical treatments. Talk it through with your GP and make sure your closest supporters know your wishes. There's more information online: *nhs.uk/conditions/end-of-life-care/advance-decision-to-refuse-treatment*

Pets
Who will look after your pets if you need to be looked after away from home, and after you have died? Do you need to introduce them to their future carers so they can get to know each other while you're able to give advice?

Keeping people informed
Who would you like to visit you, and who would you like to keep informed but without them visiting? Is there a list of contacts your supporters can use to make sure your friends are updated, and also to let them know about funeral arrangements?

Peaceful-place kit
What would you like around you as the end of your life approaches? I've seen a lot of people arrange their precious things around them. This includes photographs of dear ones and pets; a cat on the pillow or a dog under the bed; the comfort of a familiar perfume or aftershave; scented candles or incense sticks; playlists featuring poetry, theatre, talking books, music of all genres; recorded messages from friends and family; specific flavour requests, such as "no liquorice" or "plenty of strawberries", gin and tonic ice cubes and chain tea-drinking; comfortable fabrics such as favourite PJs, home-made blankets, a treasured scarf, and reminders of loved ones, including photographs of those who have died and videos of family on the other side of the country or the world. What's on your list?

Farewell letter
There's a farewell letter template in my book, *With the End in Mind*, that readers are welcome to copy and use. I've heard from people who have used them to send their last messages to loved ones, and also from families who used them to tell the dying person exactly how and why they are so loved. What a lovely thing to do.

Wishing you well with your planning.

"What matters most to you? Is it a place? People? A pet? A way of life? A spiritual practice?"

Saying goodbye

"At least two kinds of courage are required in ageing and sickness. The first is the courage to confront the reality of mortality – the courage to seek out the truth of what is to be feared and what is to be hoped. But even more daunting is the second kind of courage – the courage to act on the truth we find"
American surgeon, public health researcher and author Atul Gawande, *Being Mortal*

We're fascinated by stories of death, but there's still so much anxiety when it comes to the idea of accepting our own mortality. Even if we can get our heads around funeral planning, the concept of saying goodbye to our lives and embracing that final moment can often be too distressing to consider.

So how do we make the thought of saying goodbye easier to discuss? Firstly, it's crucial to relax about it – contrary to superstition, talking about it won't make it happen any sooner.

As with everything involved in planning what happens when you die, it's important to remember that there's no right or wrong way to say goodbye. You might hope to be able to say it face to face, to the people you care about most, but as the era of COVID-19 has proved, this isn't always possible.

So, yes, your farewell will depend on the circumstances of your death. And while some of us won't have the chance to communicate it in person, what we leave will count just as much. Our legacy – in whatever form it comes – is something that can live on and last longer than any words we might have prepared. However, for those in care or with advance warning, saying goodbye might mean considering what matters most to you and celebrating it one last time – a trip to your favourite place with your favourite person, a karaoke session with your friends at your bedside, or being surrounded by creature comforts. This goodbye isn't about "wrapping up", but it can be the cherry on top of the colourful life you've led.

You may be curious about the physical and emotional changes that happen, too. As you approach the end, your body will look and feel different. Physical changes you might notice include a severe lack of appetite and a chronically dry mouth, as well as restlessness. It's also very common to stop feeling the need to socialise and talk to people. Think also about whether you'd like to incorporate any religious, spiritual or personal rituals into your final days – these can help you to create an atmosphere that reflects your personality and the life you've lived.

Every farewell you make can help you come to terms with the fact that you will be leaving this world – and shape how you approach this physically, emotionally and spiritually. Learning about the inevitable changes is part of being prepared and can help you to cope with the thought of your own death. And even when you've finally let go and your heart has stopped beating, all those amazing moments you've experienced will live on forever.

Words at the Threshold

Linguist Lisa Smartt was fascinated by the words her terminally ill father was uttering as he was nearing the end of his life, and so started transcribing his conversations. This led to her investigating the final words of people on their deathbeds and the result was the 2017 book *Words at the Threshold*, which explores the linguistic patterns across 2,000 utterances from 181 people in their final days.

Writing your goodbye letter

"When you're confronted with the prospect of your own death, putting your feelings into words can be one way to find clarity about the life you've lived"

"Acceptance is found only by wholly inhabiting our denial. Contemplating death is really contemplating resistance, and for a long time. How do we get ready to die? We start with not being ready. We start with the fact that we are afraid. A long, lonesome examination of our fear. We start by admitting that we are all future corpses pretending we don't know"
Sallie Tisdale, *Advice for Future Corpses (And Those Who Love Them): A Practical Perspective on Death and Dying*

When was the last time you wrote someone a letter? No, not an email or a WhatsApp message, but a good old piece of writing that involved putting pen to paper. While somewhat obsolete now, and barely present in our everyday lives, letters can be a powerful tool for helping us to deal with our own mortality. It's a centuries-old form that allows us to speak directly to our loved ones when approaching the end of life.

When you're confronted with the prospect of your own death, putting your feelings into words can be one way to find clarity about the life you've lived. Before embarking on this, though, there are a few handy guidelines and resources to consider that will help you to put even the most difficult feelings onto paper. Firstly, of course, decide on the person you're writing it for – it could be a family member, a partner or a friend, a community, or it might even be yourself. While writing the letter, make sure to think about the way the person you're addressing it to makes you feel, as well as some specific moments you've experienced together. Don't limit yourself to a letter format – it could be a poem, a drawing, an essay or maybe a diary entry reflecting on your past, present and future.

In case you need some ideas or prompts for what you might like to say when writing your final words, Sallie Tisdale's book *Advice for Future Corpses (And Those Who Love Them): A Practical Perspective on Death and Dying* has suggestions you can follow. Another great source of inspiration might be the late filmmaker and artist Derek Jarman, whose series of personal-diary entries written towards the end of his life got bound into *Modern Nature*, arguably one of the most significant pieces of queer British literature of the 20th century. But this isn't homework – a goodbye letter might only need to be a few sentences and a doodle. Whatever you decide to do, remember that it might be impossible to say or show everything you want to. Your letter doesn't need to be a definitive autobiography, but it can be some of the greatest hits you've created with the person it's addressed to. Writing something like this isn't just about making the other person feel good, though – it can also be used as a coping mechanism for the writer. In therapy, composing a farewell letter is a mourning technique used to overcome difficult life situations, such as losing a job or ending a relationship. It can help us to process complicated emotions caused by these big events, and may nudge us towards coming to terms with or finding new ways to express certain truths. Known as a piece of "transactional writing", this letter might also be a chance to say thanks, to forgive or to ask for forgiveness.

And then there's the question of what to do with your goodbye letter. Do you keep it safely stored in a place where the addressee (if there is one) will find it once you've died? Deliver it in person, if that's an option? Put it in the post? Perhaps you don't want it to be seen by anyone but you. Obviously the choice is up to you, but bear in mind you might not get the response you expected – it's an emotional moment, so don't be offended if the person you've written your letter to chooses to read it in private, or finds it too hard to read straightaway but may cherish it as a keepsake in the years to come.

Putting pen to paper
Writing a letter to a loved one who is dying can be a great way to say goodbye. In 2016, Leonard Cohen wrote a goodbye letter to his former girlfriend Marianne Ihlen, the subject of his 1967 song "So Long, Marianne". In the poignant missive, delivered to her deathbed, the songwriter wrote: "I'm just a little behind you, close enough to take your hand."

Your voice

While most people can't stand the sound of their own voice, there's incredible power in hearing that of someone you loved after their death. And in this era of apps and social media, there's no reason your best friend should be restricted to calling your voicemail in order to hear you speak one last time. Thanks to the technologies built into our everyday lives through smartphones and other devices, voice notes are now as easy to record as letters are to write. And as with letters, there are certain tips and tricks that will make the process of creating and sharing your audio or video farewells easier.

According to the psychologist Elaine Kasket, these posthumous audio messages should be treated as an extension of things you've said and done during your lifetime. You may wish to record your own goodbye note or just leave your phone on the coffee table during random chats with loved ones.

After deciding on the message you wish to leave and recording it, make sure to find the right medium to share it through. If you're not tech savvy, ask someone to help with the recording. In order to avoid your message being stuck in digital limbo, it's best to either send it directly or to a person who can pass it on. Another option is to use digital legacy services, which will then be responsible for sharing your message after death, but make sure to do plenty of research and get help with navigating tech-company protocol through the field's leading body, the Digital Legacy Association.

However, an audio message doesn't have to just be a recording of your voice. Phone apps such as Soal and Replika are taking this notion one step further by developing interactive memory banks to preserve your voice. While Soal helps to create soundtracks to imagery in your camera roll by overlaying it with sounds, voice recordings or just your favourite music, Replika enables you to build a virtual version of yourself by exchanging hundreds of text messages with an AI bot that then learns your approach to different subjects. That may sound too gimmicky or unnecessarily 21st century to some, so feel free to keep things simple.

Songs and music are also a great way to pass on your voice to loved ones and future generations. Based in Yorkshire, The Swan Song Project is a brilliant service that allows those approaching the end of their lives to write and record an original song with the help of a professional songwriter as your final performance – no previous musical experience necessary. Read an interview with the project's founder, musician Ben Buddy Slack, on page 44.

"There's an incredible power in hearing the voice of someone you loved after their death"

Your legacy

"By moving ourselves away from centre stage, we become aware of the vastness of creation and the universe: our personal part in the scheme of things becomes insignificant and our births and deaths become as important as the life cycle of a butterfly or an ant"
Bertrand Russell, philosopher

According to the *Cambridge English Dictionary*, the term legacy is primarily defined as "money or property that you receive from someone after they die". This might only be a definition, but it's undeniable that the pressure of leaving some money behind can loom large when you start thinking about what will happen when you leave this world. However, it's important to remember your legacy is more than the total financial value of your possessions – it's also words, photo albums, family heirlooms, good deeds, wild nights out, stories, laughter and other intangible moments. Each life is full of nuance and immeasurable impacts, so think of your legacy as an individual sum of the things and ideas you deem as representative of you and wish to leave behind.

According to Dr Kathryn Mannix's checklist (page 112), it's important to create a list both of the things that matter to you and the people you trust to be the flagbearers of your legacy, whatever that might be. For some people, their legacy will be their life's work – the effect they had on their community as a teacher, or the ideas lying in that unpublished novel in their drawer. For others, family is important, and passing down their family history and traditions. You might want a bench or a street named after you – while it will cost you roughly £1,300 for a memorial spot in Westminster, London, the latter might prove a bit trickier, as it requires a whole new street to be built first. There's also the option of using your inheritance to fund a scholarship or charity that supports a cause you care about, or to start a non-profit organisation of your own. And there are many other ways of leaving behind some money for good, as outlined on page 25.

Artistic expression is another element you can utilise when considering your legacy as you face the end of your life. What about creating an artwork? A painting, a mural, a quilt or something more experimental? You might want to work on a scrapbook of drawings, words and photographs, or perhaps a cookbook of all your favourite recipes that can be enjoyed for years to come. Re-evaluating your legacy can be an opportunity to think of the people you've known as you face the end of your life – who has made an impact on you? Who have you made an impact on? Try making a list of 40 people who have touched your life – you may be surprised by who comes to mind. It's also a chance to look back at the highlights you experienced. Your legacy can be as big or small as you wish, but don't let any societal expectations affect the process of defining it.

Unusual legacies
When he passed away in 1982, the Polish composer André Tchaíkowsky left his skull to the Royal Shakespeare Company to be used as a stage prop – as indeed it was by David Tennant when he played Hamlet in Gregory Doran's 2008 production. Similarly, in the US, stagehand John Reed requested in his will that his skull be gifted to Philadelphia's Walnut Street Theatre, where he had worked for decades in the 1800s.

Your digital death

"*Of course, there's also the option of continuing your journey in the online realm post-mortem. Scheduling tweets for years into the future*"

Tweet, text, email, download, post, story, share…
As we continue to spend a huge chunk of our waking hours online (25.1 per week on average in the UK), it's inevitable that an increasing part of our identities has been uploaded into the digital realm. Instead of photo albums there's your Instagram account and the numerous selfies stuck in your smartphone's camera roll, and in place of the box of letters your grandmother kept in her attic, your Gmail account is overflowing with cherished in-jokes shared with your pals and newsletters you accidentally subscribed to six years ago. But what happens to all of this when you're gone? The remnants of your virtual self don't just vanish when you physically shuffle off your mortal coil. Digital afterlives are very much a natural consequence of the 21st century, and therefore an important aspect to think about when you're reflecting on what you're leaving behind.

The main question is, do you want your digital footprint to be eradicated or not? Before making this big decision, it might be helpful to read *All the Ghosts in the Machine: The Digital Afterlife of Your Personal Data* by Elaine Kasket, in which she asks all the right questions about dying in the digital age and provides a plethora of answers. The key thing to remember is that you shouldn't leave things to the last minute – whatever decision you make, it's important to share it with someone you trust, along with all the information that will help the nominated person access your accounts once you've left this world. Netflix, Amazon, Twitter, Facebook, Instagram, Gmail, LinkedIn, even online banking… The list goes on and needs to include all the digital services you use in your everyday life without even thinking about them – remember, they will exist even when you no longer do.

With the mission of simplifying this process, the Digital Legacy Association has created a template for a social media will, which isn't a legally binding document, but rather a part of your personal statement that enables you to clarify what you want to do with each account, as well as who you want to manage it.

To delete accounts on most major social media platforms, as well as the email or Dropbox of someone who passed away, the next of kin will primarily need a copy of the death certificate along with a signed statement. Many of these digital services also offer the option of compressing your profiles into downloadable content that can then be part of your physical legacy. Who knows, one of your tweets just might end up in the history books one day. Interestingly, only 27% of social media users in the UK want their profiles to be deactivated after their death.

Of course, there's also the option of continuing your journey in the online realm post-mortem. Scheduling tweets for years into the future or developing a bot that will do it for you are both legitimate options that are easily accessible. Facebook allows for your profile to be "memorialised" after you die by turning your wall into a page where people can leave comments.

The Digital Legacy Association has detailed guidelines for each big platform, as well as a checklist for leaving your mobile phone (and everything that's on it) behind. However, don't get wrapped up in polishing your digital legacy to perfection – just like during your lifetime, the people who really matter will remember the good times you shared in person rather than the things you tweeted.

Your digital afterlife
Companies such as MyWishes, Gone Not Gone and SafeBeyond help you to leave goodbye messages that are posted to social media accounts after your death, giving you an afterlife in the digital realm. Posts can be scheduled for key dates in the future, too, meaning you can still play a part in birthdays, anniversaries and holidays from beyond the grave. You might want to warn your loved ones of your plans in advance, though.

Pets and death

"Heaven goes by favour. If it went by merit, you would stay out and your dog would go in"
Mark Twain, writer

With recent figures indicating that there are about 51 million pets spread across 12 million households in the UK, the conversation about what to do with your favourite non-human is an important part of planning your farewell. And while they might be your best friend, a pet is legally considered to be the property of their owner, which means they'll need to have a new home arranged for them through your will after your passing. For that reason, it's essential to have these discussions with the people you're thinking of leaving your furry, feathered or scaled companion with in advance. You might think someone is a dog person because they like to walk yours from time to time, but have you checked whether their partner is allergic?

Almost a third of people in the UK have made provisions for a pet in their will. This is a fairly simple process, and you can even name a substitute beneficiary in case the first is unable or unwilling to take on your pet in the event of your death. But remember that having a pet can be expensive – the average lifetime cost of owning a dog is about £17,000. Though you can't leave money in your will to a pet, setting up a discretionary trust is a good way of securing the funds for the chosen guardian. Alternatively, you can also leave a cash gift that would cover the cost of food and vet's bills through your will.

If you don't have anyone in your close circle who can take care of your pet, you can register them with one of the charities that help to take care of and rehome pets after their owners' death. The Cinnamon Trust works with the elderly across the UK with the mission to respect and preserve the treasured relationship between owners and their pets. Through its large network of more than 17,000 community volunteers, it arranges everything, from walking the dogs of housebound owners to fostering the pets of those who are hospitalised or have died. Other charities that offer pet-care schemes include the RSPCA, Cats Protection, the Dogs Trust and the Blue Cross. This is something else not to be left to the last moment, though – make sure to plan ahead so that your BFF's future will be as happy as it was when you were there with them.

Wealthy pets
Though pets can't inherit money directly, trusts can be set up for their care, meaning wealthy owners can ensure the continuation of the lavish lifestyles of their beloved pets after they pass away. When he died in 2019, the iconic fashion designer Karl Lagerfeld reportedly left a sizeable chunk of his £153 million fortune for the care of his Birman cat, Choupette, who has her own agent, personal chef and Instagram account. Another wealthy pet was the English cat called Blackie, who reportedly inherited a £7 million fortune from his owner, a wealthy antiques dealer, in 1988.

Your epitaph

How would you like to be remembered when you depart this world? This is an opportunity to think about your epitaph. If you had to pick one phrase to leave behind that sums up how you lived your life and the lasting impact you've had on the people around you, what would it be?

Even amidst fierce flames the golden lotus can be planted

Sylvia Plath

True to his own spirit

Jim Morrison

Against you I will fling myself unvanquished and unyielding – O Death!

Virginia Woolf

Free at last. Free at last. Thank God Almighty. I'm Free at last

Martin Luther King, Jr

What phrase would you
like on your tombstone?

_____

_____

_____

_____

_____

What one thing would you
like to be remembered for?

_____

_____

_____

_____

_____

Interview with
Carole Walford
Chief clinical officer of Hospice UK

With her extensive experience in palliative care, Hospice UK's chief clinical officer discusses why dying matters

A senior clinician with rich experience in the field of palliative and end-of-life care, Carole Walford started her career as a nurse at London's St Bartholomew's Hospital, working with people who, at that time, were given the diagnosis of being terminally ill. More than 34 years later, she has become a figurehead for the sector, leading Hospice UK's clinical team to support and train those specialising in end-of-life care in hospitals, hospices, care homes and the community.

Q **What took you into the field of palliative care?**
A I trained as a nurse in the early 1980s and quickly became a sister on a haematology ward, looking after people with blood cancers mainly. The treatments were still developing at that point and we were still learning a lot about what worked and what didn't. People would come in for treatment and care and sometimes the treatments wouldn't work, and it would then be about looking after them until they died.

Palliative care in that setting was often handed over to the skill of the nursing team. It was very much, "It's up to you and your team sister, you look after them." I knew that we had to do more for these people. At that point, there were the beginnings of palliative care and end-of-life care teams in the acute hospitals, bringing hospice principles to hospitals and community settings. I was successful in my application to join the palliative care team at St Bartholomew's Hospital in London. We worked in the hospital and community, supporting people with the principles of good end-of-life care, and holistic care, which basically means physical, emotional and spiritual support, as well as all the practical and medical things that need to be sorted out when someone is no longer going to be cured of their illness.

Q **What are some of the key principles of end-of-life care?**
A I believe there's an acuteness to offering good end-of-life care. We only have one chance to get it right. There were specialist skills I needed to [have to] work in haematology and to give chemotherapy, and similarly there's a specialist knowledge and approach to looking after people at the end of their lives. Good communication and listening are essential. It's important to ask people questions like, "What matters to you?", rather than, "What's the matter with you?" This isn't a question just to be asked in the last weeks and days, it's asked at the point of diagnosis, especially if it's known that life

is going to be shorter than it could have been. When I was a nurse specialist, I would say to people as an opening question, "How are things?", because they'll tell you what's at the top of their head. If you ask about pain, they'll tell you about pain, but they might not tell you that their biggest worry at the moment is who's looking after their budgie at home or how they're going to tell their children what's happening.

In this job, we're in a privileged position to be alongside people as they face their mortality, offering support at a time of personal challenge and helping them to find their way through their reflections to make their own choices. Our role is to help them by giving them the tools and information they need to make the decisions that are right for them. You might have someone who decides that they want to die at home, and you might look at that situation from an assessment [point of view] and think, "Oh gosh, I'd far rather you were safer somewhere else," but you support them as far as you can to die where and how they wish. There's a quote from Dame Cicely Saunders [the nurse, medical social worker and physician who founded the modern hospice-care movement] that says, "We add days to life and life to days." Hospice care isn't about a building or care setting, it should be a living movement, responding to society and supporting people to live and die in ways that they choose.

Q **You've worked in the field of palliative care for more than 30 years. What can you share with us about dying?**
A We have two certainties in life – we know that we'll be born and we know that we'll die. Life and death are intrinsic to nature and the human condition, but we don't know the time frames of when they're going to happen. For me, it's about being aware of the value of the everyday, taking joy in your relationships now and looking at what we have today. It's something we've all learnt in the COVID-19 pandemic, to stop and smell the roses a bit.

What I can share with you about dying is that we all do it our own way. When you're expecting a baby, you might have a beautiful birth plan with a birthing pool, music, candles, a partner rubbing your back, but then a situation changes and you end up having an emergency C-section. It's [the same with death]. We're living with the fact of an unknown time frame – sometimes we can plan and anticipate, at other times people don't have that opportunity. That's quite a big, grown-up thing to think about, however old you are.

Q **Within the hospice movement, how are people's different end-of-life wishes met?**

A It comes back to what matters to you. Right now, it's about society having a voice and the importance of having a choice about how you die. Young people in their twenties and thirties are quite vocal about what they want – it's a generation that openly talks about identity and gender and has [spearheaded the] Black Lives Matter movement. They're vocal, so it's a great opportunity to have conversations about what's important to them about the way they live and the way they would want to die, as well as their wider belief systems.

Different cultures also have different values around end-of-life care and death. Some see admission or referral to a hospice or hospital as failure, as they believe they should be looking after their own communities. Some see death as part of the natural cycle of life and have rituals associated with this that are important to those left behind. It's about understanding what's important to each person. This has been one of the big challenges of the COVID-19 pandemic, as people haven't been able to be there with loved ones when they died, and laying-out ceremonies and funerals have taken place without people being able to attend. That's a concern for the bereavement care of the families afterwards, because they haven't been able to fulfil the usual rituals that enable them to say goodbye.

Q **Working with a coalition of individuals and organisations, Hospice UK runs the Dying Matters campaign. What are its main aims?**

A We're a campaign to change public attitudes towards death, dying and bereavement and to promote and actively engage the general public in starting those conversations that are difficult. It's [about creating] that open culture to talk about death and dying, listening to people and harnessing their stories to make the experience of death relevant and relatable. It's pointless talking to someone in their twenties about what it's like to die at 70 or 80. They want to know what happens if they get advanced cancer in their twenties, what if the relationship with their husband falls apart or their identity or sexuality is compromised. The 17th-century French writer François de La Rochefoucauld said, "Death, like the

sun, cannot be looked at steadily." Though the sun is there, and you feel its warmth, you can't and don't want to look at it the whole time. It's the same with death, it's always there, and there are times to talk about it and times not to. I think it's about making the most of living as well as having an open culture where people feel listened to and supported to talk about death.

Q **How early should we start those conversations about death?**

A I don't think there's anything wrong with talking about death in schools. Especially in this current COVID-19 climate, lots of teachers are going to be facing students who have lost Granny or an auntie or uncle. Death is part of life and, through the joy of having a goldfish or a hamster, children learn that life is finite. There's a lot of information on the Hospice UK and Dying Matters websites, as well as [the site for the children's palliative care charity] Together for Short Lives, to support parents and teachers to have those conversations.

Q **What are some of the most common final wishes that people have at the end of their lives?**

A It's usually about wanting to leave a legacy – parents wanting to write letters to their children for their future 18th birthdays – and there are often quite a lot of weddings, too! Sometimes there are reconciliations between families and sometimes not – sometimes people are born angry, they live angry and they die angry, and you're not going to see the television-drama tearful reunion before a final breath. At the end of life, there's definitely a sharpening of focus, a redefining of what's important. In terms of the children's sector, there's the Winston's Wish [childhood bereavement] charity and Dreams Come True, through which children [with life-limiting conditions] can go to Disneyland or meet their favourite football star. People often ask to eat their favourite foods, maybe taste a malt whisky from Scotland, visit a special place or even sometimes have an anniversary brought forward in the calendar. It's just the simple pleasures, and again, adding "life to days".

"For me, it's about being aware of the value of the everyday, taking joy in your relationships now and looking at what we have today"

"I don't think we co[n] the optimism and co[n] confront other subje[ct] we're nervous about But the fact of the m[atter] can't avoid death, it's

Journalist and broadcaster John Stapleton, from an interview as part of Lost for Words, Royal London's 2020 exhibition in collaboration with RANKIN

*front death with
nfidence that we
cts with because
upsetting people.
atter is that we
not an option"*

Interview with
Judith Moran
Director of Quaker Social Action

The director of the anti-poverty charity speaks about Down to Earth, an initiative that seeks to battle funeral poverty

As director of the 154-year-old anti-poverty charity Quaker Social Action (QSA), Judith Moran has overseen many successful projects, though one holds special significance for her. Launched in 2010, Down to Earth began as a grassroots initiative to support members of the community who were facing funeral poverty, but it soon became clear that this was by no means an issue restricted to those living around QSA's home base of east London. Now, mostly through word of mouth and some clever digital signposting, Down to Earth has become a national helpline. Its small team helps those struggling to pay for a funeral by offering advice on how to keep costs down and navigate funeral planning, and by giving gentle, caring guidance on how they can make sure the funeral is affordable but still meaningful.

Q You're part of a grassroots organisation that offers advice to low-income individuals and families who are struggling to pay for funeral costs. Why aren't funerals affordable?

A The challenge, if you live in poverty, is often that your finances are precarious. You're just about managing and it's touch and go. The thing that's difficult or catastrophic is if you have an unexpected expense. This could be a small thing, like needing to buy new school shoes for your children or having to replace your cooker. Or it could be a larger thing, like a funeral. Where do you go for help if you need to pay for a funeral? We did some research and realised that the cost of funerals was going up and the support from the government was plateauing.

As a country we're not very funeral savvy – why would you know how much a funeral costs? What do we know about funerals before we have to plan one? You know how much a washing machine should cost because you see them in shops or know someone who's bought one, but you don't walk past a funeral directors and see prices in the window. The industry is still shrouded in this mystery. We felt the best help we could offer was providing advice for people to think about the cost of the funeral, to get the cost down and get more financial support. Initially, because it was such a weird idea, we thought no one would come! We started with the local hospice in Tower Hamlets, where we're based. Now, having had no intention of growing, we are a national helpline.

Q Why do you think the Down to Earth initiative has had such wide appeal?

A Death is an unspoken subject and so is money. It's a double whammy – death and money are the two things we least like to talk about in our society. And where do they interact? In funerals. When somebody has to sort out a funeral it's at precisely the time they've got all of these emotional challenges connected with grief. They're vulnerable, paralysed and uncertain, and a little bit like a rabbit caught in headlights. One of the phrases used quite often is "a good send-off". It seems to matter so much to people that they give someone a good send-off, and people will be very sensitive about being judged for not giving someone a good send-off when it's not really clear what a good one is. We conflate the idea of a good send-off with a "spend-off", and we think we have to spend a certain amount of money. Funerals are usually held within a week [of the person dying], so a funeral director needs to understand the family's wishes and make it happen. But there's a cost to that and that's not always affordable. At Down to Earth we try to understand what somebody really wants, what they need and what they can afford. You don't have to have all of these big things, actually – what matters are those feelings and that sense of saying goodbye to someone in a dignified way.

Q Down to Earth is working to change the industry as well, right?

A We've worked with some amazing funeral directors who've gone above and beyond the call of duty to support people. For many it's a vocation. But at Down to Earth we believe the funeral industry is one that needs to open up. We don't tend to use the word "consumer" in the context of buying a funeral but it can be helpful to do so – as consumers we tend to be more aware of our rights to demand and expect a good service. So, yes, we wanted to work with the industry and influence the government and see what we can do.

Have you ever thought about how there's no minister of death? There's nobody responsible for the one thing that's guaranteed to happen to all of us. As people say, there are only two things certain in life – death and taxes – and think how big HMRC is. The lack of an overall strategy leads to regional differences, which is why public health funerals can be a bit of a postcode lottery, depending on what your local authority allows or doesn't allow for your funeral. We absolutely felt that the industry was doing a good job in many ways but could be more open, less paternalistic and certainly could have greater price transparency. So we set up the Fair Funerals pledge and asked funeral directors to sign up for free.

Q How does the Fair Funerals pledge affect everyday people?

A Many people struggle to pay for a funeral and it used to be that if you wanted the cheapest funeral you sort of had to ask for it. It's like going into a restaurant you can't really afford, being given the menu and having to ask, "Have you got anything that's really cheap?" How would that make you feel? The Fair Funerals pledge simply asks funeral directors to display all of their prices upfront and in all of their literature – that felt reasonable. We created an interactive map and got a huge swathe of funeral directors signing up across the UK. We're only in this game to protect people who would end up in debt and distress as a result of not being able to pay for a funeral.

Q Can you give some examples of good and bad practices for public health funerals?

A The starting point is how you find out about them. Most people need to ring their local authority or look on the website for a number. Then it's about the kind of response you get when you get through to somebody. Sometimes you get through to someone who is warm, kind and welcoming, and sometimes you don't. Good practice is real clarity about what is and isn't permissible and how flexible councils can be. The best practice is when it's really easy to find out how to get in touch, you're dealt with compassionately all the way through, you absolutely get the ashes, it's not a stigmatising experience and the whole thing is handled really delicately. The opposite of that is it's impossible to find out how you access them, you're told [only] what you can't do and have, including about the ashes, and you're dealt with like you're a burden.

Q Is whether to embalm the body or not an issue?

A A funeral director we know told us about how she talks about embalming to people, which was really helpful. She explained how the view that it's the norm buys into this idea that the person is somehow still there, because they kind of look like they're there, which is a real comfort for some people. And there can be a fear that if you look at somebody who hasn't been embalmed it's going to be horrific. This funeral director said she helps people understand that, instead, [decomposition] is a really gentle and natural process, and helps people reframe their thinking. Someone who is cynical about embalming would say it's a nice little earner for the funeral industry. Yet it's actually quite an invasive process and I think if this were spelled out, a lot of people would say "Don't bother." But of course, all options are sad for the bereaved family to think about in the moment. Like all things related to dying, it's much easier to think about these things when you're not immediately facing them.

Q Why do you think we struggle to talk about death and funerals in advance?

A It's so important to know that the sky doesn't fall in if you talk about death. You don't jinx things if you talk about death. There's a certain amount of superstition and suspicion, and we'd all benefit from more down-to-earth discussions about death. We'd all benefit from being better informed about funerals before being faced with them. You're so vulnerable when you're bereaved, and anything that gives people a bit more knowledge or confidence is really valuable – they're all little bricks of support. And let's face it, unless we die very young, we're all going to be bereaved and organising a funeral at some point – it's about being as well-equipped as we can be to face that.

Public health funerals
A public health funeral is a no-frills funeral that's paid for by local councils for people who have died in poverty with no next of kin, or who have relatives who are unable or unwilling to make funeral arrangements. Between April 2018 and April 2019, local councils in the UK spent a total of £6.3 million on public health funerals.

"It's so important to know that the sky doesn't fall in if you talk about death... There's a certain amount of superstition and suspicion, and we would all benefit from more down-to-earth discussions"

TV presenter Gloria Hunniford,
from an interview as part of
Lost for Words, Royal London's
2020 exhibition in collaboration
with RANKIN

"I believe that when you los
sense of loss that you can e
lost parents, I'd lost a for
all relative to the situation
to lose a child sends you ir
imaginable, and one that I
get out of"

e a child, it's the deepest

er face. I'd personally

ner husband and yes, it's

nd the person, but I think

o the darkest black hole

thought I would never

Interview with
Hasina Zaman
Funeral director and CEO of Compassionate Funerals

The funeral director and CEO
of Compassionate Funerals
talks about organising unusual
funerals, hosting a London
Death Cafe and how she copes
with an emotionally taxing career

Hasina Zaman is a funeral director and the co-founder of Compassionate Funerals. A former artist, lecturer and teacher, she opened the business in 2012 to serve the diverse communities of east London. With a person-centred ethos, Zaman and her team organise custom-made funerals shaped to individuals' wishes and different cultural traditions, which often sees her planning unique services. The team also hosts a Death Cafe, where, as part of an international network of volunteer-run support groups, founded by the late Jon Underwood in 2011, people are invited to get together to have open discussions about death and tear down "the last taboo".

Q **You're one of the few female CEOs in London working specifically within the field of death and loss. Why do you think that is?**

A I think it's partly historical, it's the way it's been. Before the turn of the [20th] century, funerals, much like births, were held within the home, and it was women who saw people into the world and out of it. It would often be the same women within that particular community who handled births and deaths. But then funerals became industrialised, alongside things like joinery and carpentry. That's how it became male-dominated. The funerals went from being in the home to outside it, and men took charge of that role.

Q **What's your approach? What does it mean to have a "compassionate funeral"?**

A It's to have compassion infused into every single process, practice and conversation. We start off with being compassionate to ourselves. It's really important, particularly during a hard situation, rather than switching into negativity around grief. It's about just being kind to yourself. When we're engaging with the bereaved, it's about being soft — soft tones in our voice, the way we move — and being tender. We spend a lot of time listening to what the bereaved are looking for, what kind of funeral the person who passed away wanted, did they leave instructions? What's this funeral going to look like? Coming from a compassionate blank space really is about having a clean slate, where everything is new. It's about empowering families in a subtle way.

Another big part of having a compassionate funeral is the care of the deceased. I'm really strict when it comes to any dressing or preparing around the deceased, or even just moving them around the mortuary. That's done silently, and we only talk in really low tones and with the highest regard.

I believe in the soul. Even when someone's dead they can hear you and feel you — why would you want to sabotage your relationship with that person, even if they aren't physically alive? When it comes to the actual funeral it's again about making sure that the family and friends receive the funeral they want. It's not about rushing — if it takes five hours, and it runs over, we just go with it.

Q **What are some unique requests you've received or funerals you've put together?**

A There's a lot that comes to mind. There was this lady who was an animator, who did Disney animations. She had an interesting ethnic background, a mixture of Italian and German. She deliberately didn't have any contact with any of her blood family. Her "new" family were creatives in and around London, and she had asked them to arrange her funeral. She was such an amazing artist and showed us drawings of how we should dress her prior to her death. She wanted to be mummified and she also created this death mask out of hair. She made her own jewellery, which was Egyptian-inspired. She had very specific instructions — there was text and visual references. We got the widest bandages you could buy, and we started with her legs, then arms, then torso. Each process was photographed, so each time I finished one, I had to take a photograph. There were really detailed instructions on how to mummify her and put all of her jewellery on. There were lots of other personal items we had to put in with her, such as a moulding of Stonehenge. But what amazed me [the most] was the jewellery — it was large and there was lots of beading — it must have taken her hours to make. It was really important that we got it right, it was like doing a piece of art, really. She trusted us to do this and we did it. As part of her funeral-planning wishes, she wanted to be buried in a natural burial cemetery in Cornwall. We had to drive at 4am to get to the cemetery. That was a very specific funeral.

We need to talk about death
Death Cafes are held as part of an international network of volunteer-run gatherings where strangers come together to talk about death over cake and tea. Established in 2011 by Jon Underwood, who died suddenly in 2017 at the age of 44, the initiative is a non-profit that aims to increase awareness of death and help people to make the most of their finite lives. To date, more than 11,750 Death Cafes have been offered across 74 countries.

Q The funerals you organise cover different belief systems. Did you have to study the traditions and practices that these require?

A Absolutely. I didn't have a clue at first. I'm really fascinated by different cultures and religions. I know about my own Muslim faith and have found out [about others] from the various communities I've worked with. There's no one cap that fits all. If you're working with the Irish community, who are very closely linked to a particular church, it's really important you follow all the funeral rites of their religion. When I started doing Hindu funerals, which I found so fascinating, I discovered not everyone follows the same practice. It's important not to make any assumptions. We can only do what's best practice and what the family feels is right, and at times the family is governed by cultural and regional practices, and this is where nuances matter.

Q You run a local Death Cafe group, which is a social safe space for people, often strangers, to come together and have an open dialogue about death. How did you get involved?

A So, the late Jon Underwood was the founder of the movement. I met him early on while setting up Compassionate Funerals. Jon encouraged me to run a Death Cafe and said, "I want you to take Death Cafe to your communities or the BAME community," and I was thinking, "OK, I'll do that." The ethos behind Death Cafe was really about dealing with the greatest taboo – how do we actually start talking about death? How can we make this a normal subject? Let's talk about the death we've experienced – what is death? What are the barriers to talking about it and experiencing it? That's how I started [holding] Death Cafes, mainly in east London.

What I find, and what's most fascinating, is that I move my position on certain things when I go to the Death Cafe. It's like a checkpoint and I don't know what I'm going to feel or think about this time round. It's like going to a mass therapy session, though it's not therapy, it's just engaging in conversations about death and dying. It's a safe space, a confidential space and at any time you feel that you want to leave, it's completely up to you. You're not under any obligation to stay. I think once you start setting the parameters – to stay as long as you want or say as much as you want, but also, just listen – you can be healed. We learn from listening. At the moment we're looking to do more targeted work around how different communities experience death, dying and loss, so I think we've evolved.

Q Does dealing with death and dying every day ever take its toll on you?

A Normally we have about 20 calls per month, but just as we went into lockdown with the coronavirus pandemic, I had around 30 phone calls in one day and it really, really affected me. I think, initially, I experienced so much of [the callers'] shock that I just went quiet and I didn't know what to do. I think, after death, shock is one of the first feelings that you experience, so I went into a bit of daze for that day but carried on. I remember the following day I just cried, but I still came to work. I thought I could either stay in bed and cry or go to work and carry on. I just cried and cried, did my meetings and cried. I didn't feel like I could just stay in bed. The work was far more important than my pain and I just needed to do this. My team saw me at my most vulnerable. They kept saying, "Why don't you go home?" I said, "No, I feel like I need to be here." I speak Bengali and a lot of these calls were from [people with] a Bengali background. Some of the families I was dealing with had only arrived in the UK recently, so I felt that my skill set was required.

Q COVID-19 aside, does the industry have an emotional impact on you generally?

A Definitely. When I've had back-to-back funerals, I tend to go away, get a massage, look after myself, go for walks. I've become quite good at self-care and am into walking and meditation. Praying makes a big difference. You put your head down to the ground and you feel completely vulnerable. I think what makes prayer good for me is it makes you feel like you're quite insignificant when all these big things are going on. It makes you very grounded. It's OK to call yourself out and say when you're feeling quite shit. We can recover.

"A compassionate funeral is to have compassion infused into every single process, practice and conversation"

Further resources

Here are some websites, articles and templates to provide you with further information and guidance on how to say goodbye to a loved one who is dying and how to plan for your own death

Talking about death and saying goodbye

Deathbed etiquette

The initiative The Art of Dying Well has a guide to saying goodbye to a loved one who's dying, based on the advice of leading palliative care consultants, nurses, chaplains and families. Since the COVID-19 pandemic, an updated version has been created for saying goodbye to a loved one when it's not possible to be there in person.

artofdyingwell.org/caring-for-the-dying/deathbed-etiquette/etiquette

artofdyingwell.org/caring-for-the-dying/deathbed-etiquette/deathbed-etiquette-and-the-coronavirus-covid-19

Saying goodbye with a song

The Swan Song Project is an organisation that supports those with terminal illnesses to write and record an original song.

swansongproject.co.uk

Talking about death and dying

The campaign Dying Matters offers practical guidance, information and resources on how to say goodbye, the importance of good listening skills, and what the dying may experience as death approaches.

dyingmatters.org/page/TalkingAboutDeathDying

Ways to say goodbye

The charity Marie Curie has put together a guide for saying farewell to a loved one without words.

mariecurie.org.uk/blog/ways-to-say-goodbye/200035

Digital legacy

In the age of the internet, the way we plan for death, say goodbye to loved ones and are memorialised is changing. Below is a list of organisations, information and guidance that explain how to manage your digital legacy.

Digital Legacy Association

An organisation that supports the general public and end-of-life, palliative and social care professionals with information about how to plan for death and grief, and remember the deceased, in the digital sphere.

digitallegacyassociation.org

Should we leave goodbye messages?

Marie Curie has a helpful article on the implications of leaving video wills and final messages for family and friends by counselling psychologist Elaine Kasket, the author of *All the Ghosts in the Machine: The Digital Afterlife of Your Personal Data.*

mariecurie.org.uk/blog/should-we-leave-goodbye-messages/273552

Social media accounts

Marie Curie also has a guide to protecting your digital legacy after you die.

mariecurie.org.uk/help/support/terminal-illness/planning-ahead/social-media-online-accounts

Social media will template

The Digital Legacy Association has a template for a social media will that helps you detail what you want to happen to your social media accounts after you die and who you'd like to appoint as your digital executor.

digitallegacyassociation.org/wp-content/uploads/2017/07/Digital-Legacy-Association-Social_Media_Will_Template-EDITED.pdf

Pets

The following organisations will be able to help answer any questions you have about how to continue the daily care of your pet if you become ill, as well as find a loving home for them in the event of your death.

Blue Cross
A charity providing support for pet owners who can't afford private veterinary treatment and help to rehome a wide range of pets, including horses.
bluecross.org.uk

Cats Protection
This is the UK's leading feline charity that rehomes cats, including in the event of ill health or death of their owners. For those who pre-register, it supplies an Emergency Cat Care Card to keep in your wallet, which tells emergency service workers who to contact so that your cat is brought into its care.
cats.org.uk

Dogs Trust
This UK-based animal-welfare charity finds new homes for dogs and also provides a Canine Care Card for your wallet, which provides information about what should happen to the care of your dog when you die.
dogstrust.org.uk

Home Forever
A programme offered by the Irish Society for the Prevention of Cruelty to Animals (ISPCA) that rehomes pets if their owner passes away.
ispca.ie/ispca_home_forever_programme

Home for Life
An RSPCA scheme that cares for and rehomes pets in the event of their owners' death.
rspca.org.uk/whatwedo/care/homeforlife

Lifetime Pet Care
The animal sanctuary Pet Samaritans offers emergency pet rescue across the UK for owners with terminal illnesses or in the case of their death.
petsamaritans.co.uk/pet-care-help-elderly-terminally-ill

Rosie's Trust
A Northern Irish charity that helps people and their pets stay together through illness and disability in old age. It has a network of volunteers across the country that helps owners with the day-to-day care of their pets.
rosiestrust.org

The Cinnamon Trust
A UK charity that has a huge national network of volunteers who help with the day-to-day care of pets. It also provides a fostering service for pets whose owners have to spend long periods of time in hospital and an adoption service in the event of an owner's death.
cinnamon.org.uk

How to write a goodbye letter

Templates and inspiration for writing a goodbye letter to a loved one, which can help people find peace before they die.

Goodbye letter template
A free template for writing a goodbye letter from palliative care doctor and author Dr Kathryn Mannix.
static.rasset.ie/documents/radio1/2020/04/farewell-letter-waived-kathryn-mannix.pdf

Last Goodbye Letters
A website that collates inspiring goodbye letters, poems, drawings and farewell tributes.
lastgoodbyeletters.com

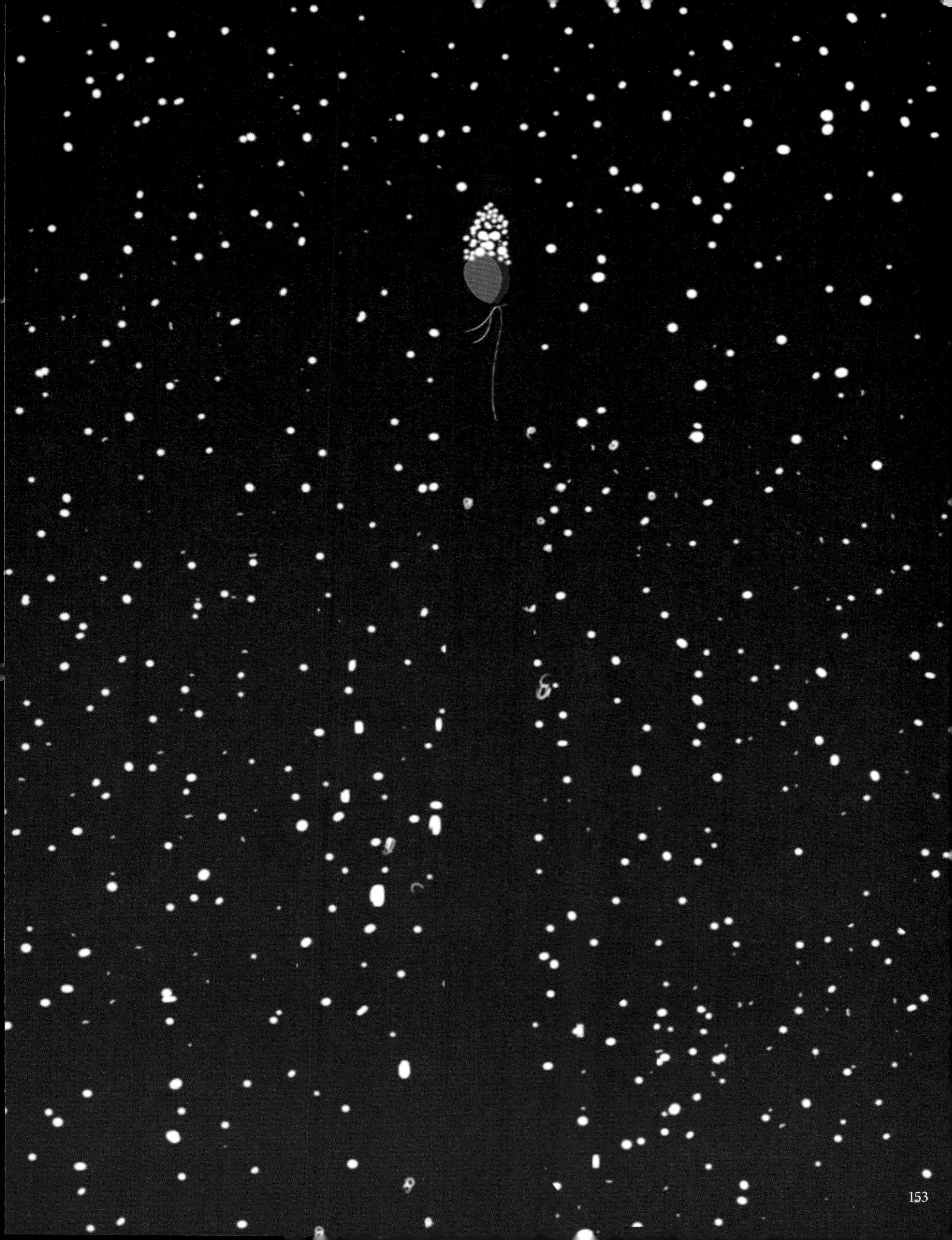

Section Four

ood

ief

How the Hindu way of grieving helped me overcome two losses

Amita Joshi

After the loss of two family members in 2017, the editor and journalist found comfort in the rituals of Hinduism's 13-day mourning period

The kettle had barely finished boiling when there was a rap at the door. Everyone's bloodshot eyes swivelled towards my grandmother's porch to see who had come already. They must have heard the news about my grandfather's death.

"We have to let them in, but we really need to get everything ready afterwards, before others come," said my grandmother, wiping her eyes on her saree. Little did I know that those few minutes when we had just returned from the hospital after saying goodbye to Dada were the only time we'd get to ourselves.

When my grandfather died unexpectedly in July 2017, and my uncle of terminal cancer in November, I wasn't prepared for the tumultuous experience that comes with "traditional" mourning. Or should I say "days of mourning", because if you are a Hindu – a Brahmin, to be specific – you observe 13 days of mourning. I had no idea what this meant, but I was about to learn very quickly that slipping back to London to pretend it was one long nightmare I'd wake up from was not it.

From that first knock on the door, it was like an electrical surge had jolted the family into action. My grandmother said we had to clear out the living room and put white sheets on the floor so people could come and sit down. We had to get a picture enlarged of my grandfather and place it at the front of the room with a garland of flowers around it and make sure the lit candle in front of it never went out.

Then the people came. Neighbours, community members, friends of friends, close friends and family who wanted to pay their respects made their way over. It's tradition to do so in those first few days. Some had walked from nearby, others drove for four hours just to spend an hour with us. It was like a surreal Indian wedding, without the rich food and devoid of laughter. Cars filled the cul-de-sac daily and the house was packed out until the evening. My immense sadness was mingled with curiosity at the sheer number of people visiting and often accompanied by wondering who half of them even were.

I couldn't understand why everyone would descend on us the way they did when our heads were still reeling. Just when we would manage to persuade my grandmother to eat something, the doorbell would ring and she'd rush off again, her plate untouched. It unnerved me. I was hardly feeling sociable, and looking presentable was completely unattainable. Didn't they think we needed some time to even register what had happened? Weren't we allowed any space?

There were so many rules and so much to do within those 13 days. Each evening we had to do prayers for half an hour. By day 13, a few days after the funeral, there was an event you had to organise at the local temple, a sort of wake a few days after the funeral that is separate from the wake itself. It was overwhelming.

But somewhere within those few days, my irritation at it all abated. The sleepless nights and constant hosting had taken its toll and I was drained. But that's when I realised I needed these people. When the first of my grandmother's friends walked through the door, gave me a hug and forcibly sat me down for breakfast, it was more welcome than ever before. Because, in that moment and from then on, I needed the help.

Each evening, when they would all read out passages of religious text and nudge us to eat khichri that they'd brought over in Tupperware, I was grateful. They'd talk about their own experiences, how it's part of our reincarnation cycle, and fleetingly it made me feel like it was a universal experience rather than an isolating one. I watched as they held my grandmother's hand and, although they couldn't take away her pain, the words gave us all strength at a time when we couldn't muster the energy to find it ourselves.

What I learnt from this extended version of mourning was that averting your gaze from death is the Western way. You don't really know which of your friends are going to be comfortable with how you (literally) cried over two dead bodies within a few months of each other. Or if they'll understand why you want to cancel plans. And discussing it with colleagues was a definite no-no, it's business as usual.

But 13 days of mourning the way my elders did made me stronger. It's painful, awkward and startles you – but facing both deaths square in the face helped. The funerals were open casket, and I watched my cousins, not even teenagers yet, bravely holding my grandfather and uncle's hands in their coffins before they were taken away. I learnt, in time, that it felt far more complete to be with them each step of the way than walk away from the hospital and never see their faces again. It felt better to see them dressed up in their finest one last time.

My friends thought it was "full on", and they weren't wrong. But what happened by the time those days were over was that I'd mourned. I'd mourned hard, without any complication. It doesn't take away the pain of losing a person, but it shows you a lot of things, like how it's OK to take time out to try to come to terms with it, rather than launching back into normality like it never happened. Even if keeping busy is your method, it reminded me that it's OK not to be functioning at the usual speed.

I deeply resented it all at first, but now I appreciate what our culture bestows on us, despite the discomfort. Grieving this way showed me a fearless and no-nonsense side of the community, which is an invaluable, powerful force for good and truly life-changing. And I'll always be grateful we did it the way we did.

"*The sleepless nights and constant hosting had taken its toll and I was drained. But that's when I realised I needed these people*"

Coming to terms with death — why do we have to die?

"There are only two days with fewer than 24 hours in each lifetime, sitting like bookmarks astride our lives; one is celebrated every year, yet it is the other that makes us see living as precious"
Dr Kathryn Mannix, *With the End in Mind: Dying, Death and Wisdom in an Age of Denial*

We aren't great at dealing with death. Deep down, we all know that the end of life is on the horizon – whether it's our own or that of someone we love. But until death is right in front of us, we've seemingly been conditioned to ignore it.

The average age that someone first loses someone close to them is 20, according to the survey *Making Peace with Death: National Attitudes to Death, Dying and Bereavement.* Its results also show that 91% of us have thought about our own mortality, some on a weekly basis, although almost 18 million people are reported to be uncomfortable about discussing death.

Why? On the face of it, dying is a scary, sad subject. The thought of no longer existing takes a certain amount of adjustment: will it be painful? Will I know what's happening? How will people cope without me? Moreover, British culture hides grief and death behind a veil of privacy, so we aren't aware of the logistical and emotional complexities – how to arrange a funeral, what happens to your body, how to apply for probate – until we have to address these issues for real, which comes at the exact moment we are grieving.

A combined lack of information and familiarity can mean we remain awkward and ill at ease when confronted with our own mortality or someone else's grief. These are universal experiences, but many bereaved people, or those facing the end of life, feel isolated because their friends simply don't know what to say.

It's up to us to make grief more of a collective process. There's a lot of power in grieving together – openly sharing stories about the dead and speaking about what grief feels like can be a huge relief for all involved. It helps to reduce the overwhelming nature of grief, the stigma surrounding it and, ultimately, the fear of our own deaths.

We can't predict what anyone's death will be like, but practitioners observe that those at the end of their lives often peacefully embrace the inevitable. Many people's deathbed reflections follow similar themes: being grateful for what they've had, the time they've spent with loved ones, and the opportunity to do what made them happy.

It's human nature to desire life, and yet knowing we die is how we fully appreciate that life. As the Swedish diplomat Dag Hammarskjöld put it: "Do not seek death. Death will find you. But seek the road which makes death a fulfilment."

Why is your grief different?

"Grief is different. Grief has no distance. Grief comes in waves, paroxysms, sudden apprehensions that weaken the knees and blind the eyes and obliterate the dailiness of life [...] Grief turns out to be a place none of us know until we reach it"
Joan Didion, *The Year of Magical Thinking*

For some, grief is wholly outward and hard to suppress. But for others, grief is internal, secretive and hidden. You might feel totally numb, wildly angry, or relatively happy and assume there's something wrong with you. In fact, all of these reactions are normal, valid and natural.

Grief doesn't look any specific way, because it's a uniquely individual response. Our bodies and brains need time to adjust to the new state of our world without this person in it.

In 1969, Elisabeth Kübler-Ross defined five stages of grief – denial, anger, bargaining, depression and acceptance – that people commonly experience when faced with dying or bereavement. More recently, David Kessler suggested a sixth stage – that of "finding meaning" as we grapple with a suitable explanation for why this loss has happened and try to stay connected to the person we've lost.

But grief isn't linear, so these stages don't appear neatly in order, and the appearance of one doesn't negate the return of another. Grief doesn't follow the "rules" of other emotions, either. It has no definable end point (although we often wish it did!) but it does seem to have two phases: an acute phase and an integrated one. During the former, it can be helpful to name some types of grief you might feel.

Anticipatory grief
When you're expecting a death, it's easy for your mind to try to prepare itself by pre-empting how the loss might affect you. This can provoke feelings of guilt for treating someone like they've already died, along with feelings of anxiety about what's to come.

Complicated grief
For some, the acute grief phase lasts for years and years, or seems to deepen in intensity as time goes on. This is known as complicated grief. More than 10% of people suffering a loss after the death of a partner or sudden death of a loved one find themselves in complicated grief.

Cumulative grief
Grief overload happens when a previous loss comes into focus while you're experiencing a current loss.

Delayed grief
Not reacting to a death at first is really common. You're subconsciously suppressing emotions in an attempt to avoid feeling the full reality of what's happened.

There are countless stories about grievers being criticised for moving on "too quickly", behaving "too normally" or crying "too much" about their loss. Some people may also question their own emotional response to a loss or fear the judgment of others. How we grieve, though, isn't a choice! It's a set of involuntary coping mechanisms.

So be sure not to inadvertently "grief shame" yourself. Remember: it's OK to cry without warning, it's OK to feel exhausted or anxious or guilty or numb. Everyone's grief looks different. Everyone reacts in their own way. Whatever you're feeling is completely valid.

Understanding grief
There are plenty of models for approaching and understanding grief in addition to the five stages outlined by the late Swiss-American psychiatrist Elisabeth Kübler-Ross. One of these is Dr Lois Tonkin's concept of "growing around grief", which suggests that while we never truly "get over" the loss of a loved one, our negative feelings will become easier to manage over time. Another is Dr Therese Rando's action-based theory, the Six Rs, which outlines tasks that will push you through different milestones in your grieving process.

Sharing bereavement

"A loss can be life-changing, and while it sadly can't be fixed with kind words or actions, there are still ways you can help to share the burden"

Supporting someone who's grieving can be tough. Their behaviours may change – someone who's usually very talkative may clam up, and someone who loves their friends dropping by unannounced might really want their privacy now. A loss can be life-changing, and while it sadly can't be fixed with kind words or actions, there are still ways you can help to share the burden:

° Daily tasks can be a good place to start. Drop off some cooked food and offer to help with difficult phone calls or paperwork.

° Be specific with your offers of help. Saying "Is there anything I can do?" places the burden of specificity on the griever. Saying "I can drive you to X if you like" invites a simple yes or no answer – much easier to handle!

° Don't say you'll provide something if you're not 100% certain you'll be able to do it. When a person has just lost a loved one, the last thing they want is to feel abandoned again.

° Let them lead the time frame of their grief. Don't push them into conversations or activities you think they're ready for.

° Basically, just *be there*. Sometimes talking isn't needed – physical companionship is enough.

Although friends and family members have the best intentions, sometimes the most relief can be found from support systems that involve people who personally understand the nature of grief. During the past decade there's been a rise in groups, clubs and meet-ups called Death Cafes, where people can gather to discuss their thoughts and feelings – both online and in the real world. You can read more about them on pages 147-148.

Bereavement Room is a podcast hosted by Callsuma Ali, in which she explores the effects of grief from a non-white perspective.

Let's Talk About Loss runs group meet-ups in 20 locations in the UK for people aged 18 to 35, along with online events, such as its monthly Bereavement Book Club.

Shapes of Grief is a blog and podcast hosted by Liz Gleeson, an Irish bereavement therapist who specialises in complicated grief. Episodes include bereavement from suicide and how to manage grief and anxiety due to COVID-19.

Siblings Grieve Too is an online community for those who have lost a sibling, helping people to find comfort, support and useful resources.

The Dead Parent Club podcast, aimed at grieving young adults, was launched by friends Kathryn Hooker and Sam Vidler, who bonded at university through talking about their own losses. The podcast's intention is to normalise the grief conversation by speaking to numerous guests.

The Griefcast podcast is hosted by the comedian Cariad Lloyd, who lost her dad when she was 15 and now interviews writers, comics and actors about their experiences of grief.

The Griefcase is a monthly meet-up run by illustrator Poppy Chancellor that allows attendees to share the ways their grief has influenced their creativity.

Attitudes to grief are undoubtedly shifting, particularly in the wake of COVID-19. We know that avoidance and grief simply don't mix. And although it can hurt like hell to face the pain of it, repressing our feelings will only make things worse in the long run. The growing online grief community has allowed people all over the world to connect through blogs, podcasts and social media hashtags, and discover that their feelings and emotions about grief are shared by many others. Finding allies, swapping stories and learning coping strategies are all hugely beneficial to shaping our long-term response to grief and truly honouring the person we've lost.

Social media can help you open up about death
Recent research suggests that posting about the loss of a loved one on Facebook can help with expressing and externalising feelings of grief to a greater degree than in face-to-face conversations, where individuals may be more likely to self-censor.

How do your beliefs affect the way you grieve?

If you practise a particular religion, the chances are your faith will bring you a good deal of comfort while grieving. The belief in a higher power might mean that you see death as an extension of physical life, just in a different state, or perhaps that your loved one is watching over you and eventually you'll be reunited. People with a strong spiritual or religious affinity often seem to be able to resolve their grief more rapidly – although a significant loss can also cause people to find that their belief in God and the afterlife has been shaken.

Buddhism

Since the faith focuses on rebirth, death is considered the most important event in your life. There are different types of Buddhism around the world, but three days of continuous worship usually follow a death, and then a cremation or burial. Memorial services are traditionally held on the third, seventh, 49th and 100th day after the death, the final one marking when family members recognise the person's soul has gone on to its next life.

Christianity

Grieving can include tending to a person's grave, visiting church more often in the year following the death and lighting candles in remembrance. In Catholicism especially, many choose to turn to the psalms of lament, which help to provide words for the pain of loss.

Is religion the key to a longer life?
A US study, published in 2018 in the journal *Social Psychological and Personality Science*, suggests that the religious may live an extra 5.64 years compared to atheists, based on analysing the details of more than 1,500 obituaries.

Hinduism

Ashes are often scattered in a river or taken to India. Following cremation, there are no prayers or rituals for 13 days because the soul is still connected to the body. Close family won't enter religious spaces during this time either. On the 13th day, a celebration marks the departure of the soul as it finds a new body to inhabit, and the family reintegrates into society. In the days that follow, as well as one year later, on the anniversary of the death, the family holds a Sraddha, a ceremony that memorialises the dead.

Humanism

The humanist approach is to accept death as a natural part of life. Without the lingering hope of reunion, humanists focus on the here and now and confront their resulting grief with what they deem to be rational compassion.

Islam

Many Islamic communities advocate a mourning period of 40 days, but depending on circumstance and custom, it could be longer; widows mourn for four months and 10 days. After this period, mourners can begin to live normally again.

Judaism

Ritual is important for the Jewish faith: the grieving process includes ritual washing of the body and allowing the grave to be filled with earth by family and friends. After the funeral, the community cares for the family while they sit Shiva – seven days of formal mourning – providing them with meals, prayer and comfort. The anniversary of the death and the religious holiday Yom Kippur are also reserved for remembering loved ones.

Collective grief

"Collective grieving is being able to connect with other people who share some of the same horror you do [...] It's experiencing grief even if you didn't lose a loved one. It's experiencing grief along with, or in honour of, people who have lost a loved one"
Camille Wortman, professor of Social and Health Psychology at Stony Brook University and an expert on grief and bereavement

Grief isn't just confined to personal losses. When a public figure dies – Princess Diana, David Bowie, Chadwick Boseman – the outpouring of collective grief is a way to share our pain. And when we experience natural disasters, terrorist attacks, wars and national tragedies, we collectively grieve the loss of our sense of safety and our trust in the world around us.

Our approach to grief has changed a lot over the past century. In the Victorian era, public mourning was pretty well established: people wore black clothes and jewellery containing the deceased's hair. But both world wars brought too many horrific deaths to mourn. Carrying on with a stiff upper lip became a point of pride, and it's only recently that we've begun to recognise the importance of being vulnerable with our grief instead of suppressing it.

It couldn't have come at a more necessary time, either. As the world heats up and climate change affects every aspect of our reality, we're collectively grieving the melting of glaciers, wildfire-ravaged land and the extinction of wildlife species. And within the turbulence of COVID-19, we're seeing what happens when the entire globe has to process a singular trauma of enormous proportions. Quite aside from the death toll, the implementation of lockdowns and social distancing has meant people haven't been able to gather together at deathbeds and funerals. It goes against every natural human impulse to not be there for each other in times of difficulty. COVID-19 is forcing us to change how we mourn.

It may feel like an overwhelming pill to swallow, but all this collective grief is actually a chance to get to grips with loss as part of the natural cycle of all things. The psychologist William Worden provides us with four tasks of mourning: to accept the reality of the loss; to work through and experience the pain and grief; to adjust to the new environment; and to find enduring connection with the deceased while moving forward with life. Perhaps COVID-19 will bring more of the world's population to view itself as a collective "us". Regardless, as we mourn a way of life that may never fully go "back to normal", it's crucial that we learn how to grieve well. Supporting each other and allowing ourselves to be vulnerable amid such uncertainty is how we prepare for whatever comes next.

"It goes against every natural human impulse to not be there for each other in times of difficulty. COVID-19 is forcing us to change how we mourn"

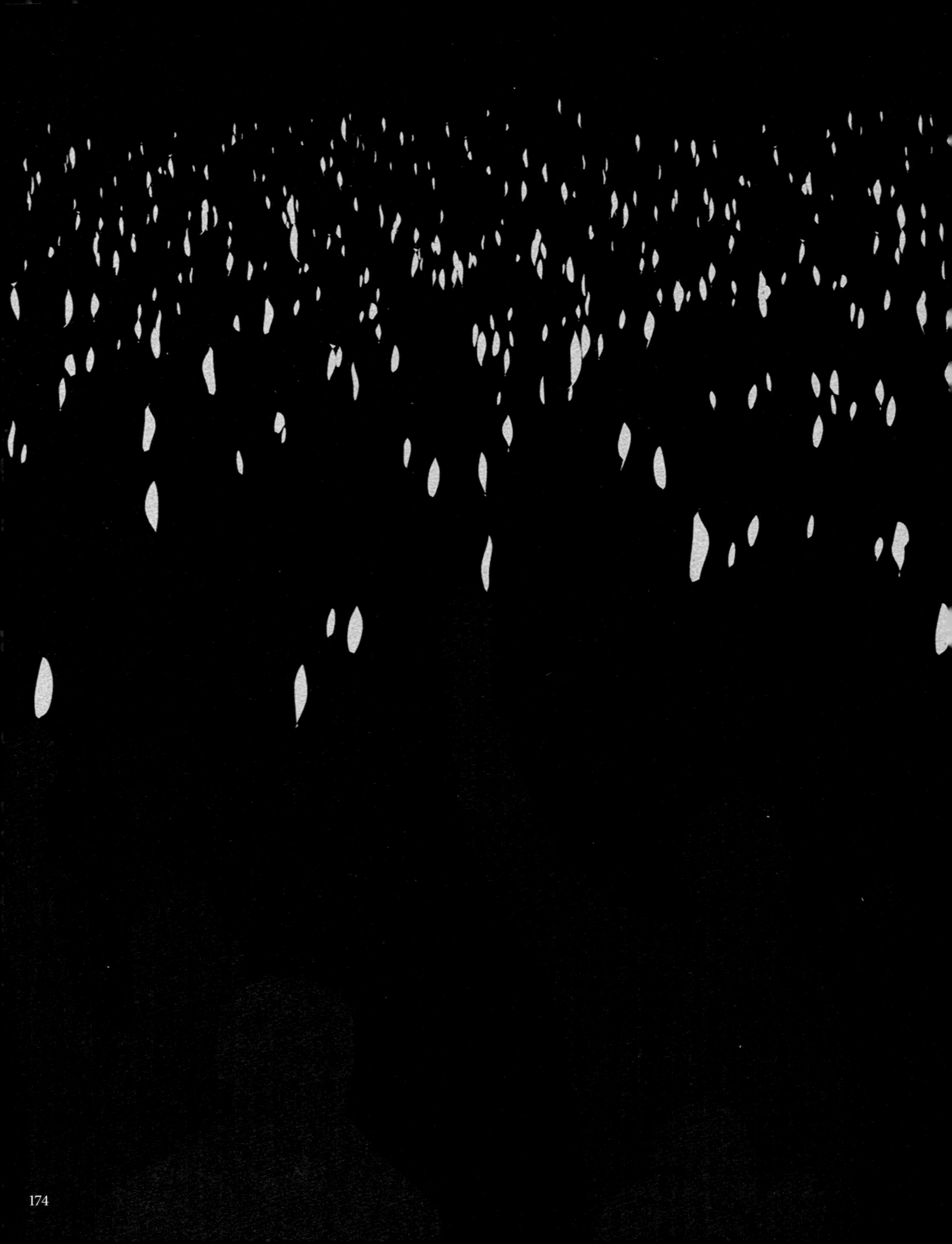

A grief reading list

Reading about grief can be a deeply cathartic process. When you see your own grief mirrored by authors in memoirs, essays and thoughtful reflections, it's a reminder that so many others have felt the same way you have. It also provides a vocabulary with which you can describe your own grief. Writing out your feelings can help you sort through difficult emotions, find clarity and closure, and even solidify the grief story you feel comfortable about sharing with others – and many bereaved people find themselves penning these stories for publication.

A Manual for Heartache by Cathy Rentzenbrink
Written after the death of her brother, Rentzenbrink describes how she learnt to live with loss in a beautifully honest and uplifting way.

Chase the Rainbow by Poorna Bell
A woman's deeply personal account of her husband's suicide, and how she found her way through the resulting grief.

I Am, I Am, I Am: Seventeen Brushes with Death by Maggie O'Farrell
An inspirational series of essays about the author's near-death experiences throughout her life and how this plays into her understanding of her own mortality.

It's OK That You're Not OK: Meeting Grief and Loss in a Culture That Doesn't Understand by Megan Devine
Grief is treated as the uncomfortable thing it is by Devine. With fiercely honest writing, she guides readers towards a place where they can live alongside their grief and even honour it.

Modern Loss: Candid Conversation About Grief by Rebecca Soffer and Gabrielle Birkner
A series of personal essays written by young adults about grieving, allowing them a space to express themselves with warmth, humour and intelligence. This book is particularly useful for teenage readers.

The Hot Young Widows Club: Lessons on Survival from the Front Lines of Grief by Nora McInerny
This memoir explores the author's response to losing her father, husband and unborn child within just a few weeks. As with her popular podcast, *Terrible, Thanks for Asking,* McInerny treats the topic of grief with humour, kindness and accessibility.

The Year of Magical Thinking by Joan Didion
A classic memoir of grief that follows acclaimed writer Didion's attempts to deal with the sudden loss of her husband.

When Breath Becomes Air by Paul Kalanithi
A physician at the end of his life reflects on what it's like to face mortality and consider what life is really lived for.

With the End in Mind: Dying, Death and Wisdom in an Age of Denial by Dr Kathryn Mannix
A palliative care practitioner for many years, Mannix seeks to open up the conversation surrounding death through a number of short stories about the end of life.

Put your feelings on page
While reading is a common coping strategy when it comes to grief, with 16% of grieving individuals in the US turning to books to process their feelings, research reports that writing is equally popular among the recently bereaved – proof that there's some truth to the notion that art can provide emotional catharsis.

What happens to the brain during grief?

Anyone who has experienced grief knows that it can be overwhelming. In order to help people to understand what they're going through, counsellors often conceptualise grief as unfolding across seven stages – but what if there's another way to think about it? Mental health experts are increasingly interested in the impact that losing a loved one can have on the brain, drawing parallels between neurological changes and the ways that many individuals act and feel when in mourning.

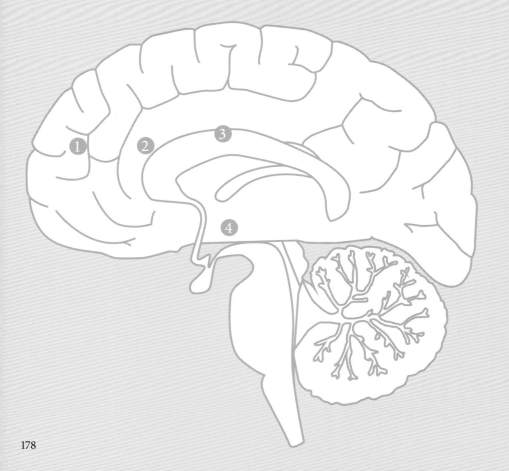

1

The prefrontal cortex
Controls decision making
Becomes underactive

2

Anterior cingulate cortex
Emotional regulator
Becomes underactive

3

The limbic system
Survival instincts
Becomes more dominant

4

The amygdala
Controls fear and sleep
Becomes overactive

People suffering from grief don't just report feelings of sadness but also of disorientation and confusion. This is proof that bereavement isn't just emotional — it affects your brain and body at a deeper level. The loss of a loved one has been compared to a brain injury, with the emotional trauma resulting in serious, possibly enduring, changes to its functionality.

Grief, and the changes to the brain that accompany it, are a protective evolutionary adaptation, allowing humans to survive when faced with this trauma. When a person is grieving, hormones are released that imitate the fight, flight or freeze response, because the body interprets the loss as an intense form of stress.

A study published in *Social Cognitive and Affective Neuroscience* claims that those in mourning experience heightened anxiety and an impaired ability to form logical thoughts.

Experts advise that, rather than fearing the way the brain changes during grief, you should embrace it, as it's a natural response. In the raw grief state, which lasts 90 days or more, a hormone is released by the pituitary gland. Named adrenocorticotrophin (ACTH), it instigates a chemical reaction, sending a signal to the adrenal glands to trigger the release of the stress hormone cortisol. During this period, the body is flooded with cortisol and the immune system may become run-down due to being in such a high state of physical alert. This is why it's common for individuals to become ill themselves upon their loved one's passing.

Bereavement can also lead to a process called neuroplasticity, where the brain rewires itself: the pathways typically relied upon take detours that shift the brain upside down to prioritise primitive functions. Due to the way your brain circuits change, the prefrontal cortex, which controls decision making, is underactive and the limbic system, which presides over survival instincts, becomes more dominant.

Other areas of the brain that are affected are the anterior cingulate cortex — the emotional regulator — which becomes underactive, and the amygdala, the determiner of how the brain responds to fear, which becomes overactive. This accounts for the sudden waves of emotion and heightened anxiety or fear that can accompany grief.

The amygdala also regulates sleep, meaning that the bereaved may find that they're sleeping too little or too much. This disruption to sleeping patterns can lead to grogginess and difficulty making decisions, commonly referred to as "brain fog".

As so much of the brain is occupied with managing emotional trauma and stress, grieving individuals find that they don't have as much cognitive flexibility as they did before the event. This means that it's difficult to be as organised or attentive as usual.

While the brain does act in specific ways when confronted with grief, each individual experiences bereavement in a different manner. The emotive response often differs depending on the intensity of the trauma and the relational patterns that have been established since childhood.

When we grieve, the parts of our brain mediating our right and left hemispheres — the areas responsible for thinking and feeling — are impaired, but these alterations aren't necessarily permanent. To overcome grief and restore neural pathways, it's important to encourage your brain to integrate thoughts and feelings. A way to do this is by connecting the loss you're experiencing with activities or specific actions. You can set your mind on the path to healing by engaging in behaviours that elicit a feel-good response.

Grief experts also believe that, in addition to restoring neural pathways, it's important to treat the effects of chronic stress (long-lasting stress that can have serious implications on an individual's health) — hence the recommendation to take time off from work or study when grieving. Treatment for chronic stress includes identifying triggers, exercising regularly, speaking with family members or friends and making sure you're getting enough sleep.

Memory box

Whether it's a family heirloom or favourite mug, everyone has special items that mean a lot. Perhaps you want your treasured possessions handed down to relatives, or maybe you have artefacts of historical significance that you would like to give to a museum or art gallery. Your memory box is a place to write down or illustrate some of the items that matter most to you, and what you want to be done with them when you're gone.

Draw or list your special objects and belongings

Interview with
Flora Baker
Writer

The British author reflects
on losing both parents in
her twenties and the comfort
she found in sharing her
experience of grief with
an online community of
adult orphans

Flora Baker lost her mother when she was 20 years old, and her father when she was 28. When an article she wrote about her experience of being an adult orphan went viral, Baker, a travel writer at the time, realised there was potential for a book. The result is *The Adult Orphan Club: How I Learned to Grieve the Loss of My Parents*, which tackles the specific feelings of adult orphanhood through a mix of heartfelt personal essays and honest, practical advice.

Q *The Adult Orphan Club is part memoir and part guidebook. Did you start writing the book with that format in mind?*

A I wrote an article a year after my dad died about how I'd lost both my parents before I turned 30 and how I dealt with the grief. Hands down, it's been the most popular thing I've ever written. I still get comments and messages about it. So I realised how much it resonated with people, particularly how I'd structured it with headers and sections the whole way through. Then, when I was writing the book, I was quite conscious of whether I should make it about grief in general or about losing your parents. Then I thought, "Screw that, it's about both." I already knew there weren't many resources on the topic, particularly for the kind of age I was. When I lost my parents, I didn't have a family of my own, a husband or anything. I was arranging [my dad's] funeral by myself and that was really shit and hard. You don't know any of the stuff you're supposed to do.

Q What are some of the practical things you wish you'd known about before losing your parents?

A A lot of stuff. There's a lot of fear about getting things wrong, from an emotional, logistical and legal standpoint. I mean, I never want to hear the word probate again. It makes my blood run cold. I still don't know if I even did it right. You suddenly have to hire a lawyer to prove stuff. Funeral arranging can be hellish. Funeral directors can prey on you like vultures. They show you a brochure of coffins and you have to spend more money to seem caring. I had a really shit funeral director. I had a call from them the day before my dad's funeral, saying, "You know there aren't going to be any flowers in the church?" I didn't know I had to order them. When I showed up with a bag of clothes for my dad to be dressed in, they sat behind the reception desk and told me to list everything in there – to itemise it! I thought I could just hand over the bag and leave. It's the most vulnerable time and you have no knowledge of what's going on or what funerals are supposed to look like. I could rant about this all day. The difficulty is that people aren't likely to read about this stuff until they're already in it. Because it's not very nice. But it's quite important.

Q Tell us about the online community of adult orphans you're part of now.

A I'm in a WhatsApp group with about 80 people across the world who've lost both their parents. We found each other on Twitter. The group is called Young Orphans and our profile picture is Orphan Annie. I met up with a few of them for the first time about a month ago and it was incredible. I forget that it started solely from being online. Some of the messages I've received on Instagram have led to friendships – I check in on [the senders] and they check in on me. It's also really emblematic of why I wrote a book specifically about losing both my parents, because it's a very specific type of grief – in exactly the way that it's a specific type of grief if you lose someone to a crime, or lose a sibling. There are so many things that are universal about the grief experience, but there are so many things that are very specific.

Q What are some of the things that are specific to the adult orphan grief experience compared to other types of grief?

A I think the biggest one for me, which I've tried to work through quite a lot, is this feeling of being unmoored or unanchored. It's grief on grief on grief. You revisit the first parent's death when you deal with the second, and then you deal with the entire loss of everyone. I have no siblings as well, so that's a biggun. Particularly if you're younger, because you haven't set up the next stage of your life – such as kids or a partner. That makes it really tough and makes you kind of rootless and anchorless. And, in my case, you then try to grab an anchor any way you can. That loss of anchor is a big thing to deal with. The loss of everything to do with family – my parents aren't here to remind me of stuff I did as a kid. I don't have anyone else saving those memories, it's just me. I'm scared I'll lose stuff. Because I can't get that information back. That's why I tell people to record their parents talking as much as they can – for their voices but also for stories. It can feel very artificial to prompt it, but I recorded every conversation I had with my dad during his last six months.

Q Is writing an important part of the therapeutic process for you?

A When I first realised something really bad was happening to my mum, I immediately started writing stuff down. I didn't think, "Oh, I want to write this down." It was automatic – "I have to keep track, I have to record it, it's happening so quickly and I'm so scared." It's a very intense, internal thing. The same thing happened when my dad became ill – I wrote a lot then. For me, the cathartic and therapeutic essence of it comes from being able to put borders around what's happening. Grief is such a formless and shapeless thing, and writing gives me a chance to kind of put a frame around it and hold it in a bit.

Q Are there any books or writers on grief that have inspired you?

A You can't beat Joan Didion. Emily Dean's book *Everybody Died, So I Got a Dog* is great, too, because she describes grief with humour! I read that book in awe.

"Grief is such a formless and shapeless thing, and writing gives me a chance to kind of put a frame around it and hold it in a bit"

"*For me the world be*
the birds singing, ca
just so loud. The phy
was what really surp
I'd lost a limb, but I
a physical part of me

came very noisy —
s going past. It was
ical feeling inside
rised me, not that
felt like there was
missing"

Sarah Abernethy-Hope,
co-founder of Billy Chip,
a charity that supports the
homeless, from an interview
as part of Lost for Words,
Royal London's 2020
exhibition in collaboration
with RANKIN

Interview with
Noel Conway

Assisted dying campaigner

The activist discusses his
campaign to change the law
in the UK to give the terminally
ill the choice to end life on
their own terms

Heavily involved with trade unionism throughout his life, Noel Conway – a former lecturer and previously a local councillor in Blackburn, now living in Shropshire – has always fought passionately for what he believes in. When diagnosed with terminal motor neurone disease (MND) in 2014, he was confronted with the legal impossibility of procuring a medically assisted death in the UK – something he describes as a "complete distortion of human rights". Joining forces with the organisation Dignity in Dying, he set out to challenge the law and, despite numerous setbacks along the way, is still applying political pressure for the right to have an assisted death.

Q **Before we talk about your campaigning work, let's rewind a little bit. What have been some of the highlights of your life so far?**

A That's one of those questions that kind of throws you. When you're 70 years of age and someone asks you, "What are the highlights of your life?", it [needs] really rather more than just a few minutes or moments to think about that. I got married at 20 or 21, my first wife was a similar age to me, and we met at church. After finishing university, I went into the further-education sector, where I remained for 36 years. I became a senior manager, running various courses and organising as well as teaching. That's been a very important part of my life, as has politics. I was quite heavily involved in politics. I became a member of the Labour Party at 14 and a local borough councillor at the age of 21, which was the youngest you could be.

Q **MND is a degenerative condition – how have your physical symptoms progressed in the years since your diagnosis in 2014?**

A I was told when I was diagnosed that I probably had between 6 and 18 months to live, which was quite a shock. Coming to terms with that was difficult for my wife and me. [Shortly after my diagnosis] I found it difficult walking more than 100 yards, and it wasn't long before I was having to rely on a wheelchair. From then on it was just a series of declining steps to where I am now – six years later, mind you, and still alive. I've now reached a stage where I'm paraplegic. I can move my head a little, I can eat, I can drink and I can talk, so in that respect I'm fairly atypical of many MND sufferers, many of whom lose their voices early on.

Q What led you to start contemplating assisted dying?

A After my diagnosis I started to think quite bleakly about doing away with myself, but not in the way that many people do, with a lot of pills. I don't know why, but I read a lot into it and came across groups like Exit [International] and I thought, "Oh, OK." Then I got to know of Dignitas [a Swiss autonomy and dignity group for assisted dying] and I thought that was much more civilised, so I joined and I've been a member ever since.

Q Under the 1961 Suicide Act, it's illegal to assist a suicide, and anyone found doing so can be jailed for up to 14 years — something you've been fighting to change. Why did you decide to campaign for assisted dying in the UK?

A When I discovered what the law was, though I already knew it in broad terms, I found this to be a complete distortion of human rights. At more or less the same time I became aware of the organisation Dignity in Dying. I liked what I read and could see that they were trying to change the law in the UK. I thought, "This has got to be the way forward." I came to the conclusion that it was very important to try to change things. They called for volunteers to disclose their story, so I sent my details off, not expecting to hear any more about it. They ended up taking it further and eventually I became the lead case in asking for a judicial review from the British Supreme Court.

Q There's been a lot of opposition to changing the law on assisted dying from disability groups who see it as potentially setting a precedent for euthanasia. How would you respond to their arguments?

A It's quite clear from some of the places that do have assisted dying, like Oregon, that it's not a slippery slope to euthanasia. Jurisdictions like the Netherlands, Belgium and Luxembourg that have euthanasia have had it right at the beginning, they made no bones about it. Assisted dying is not euthanasia, euthanasia is not on the table for the UK. I also don't think these groups speak for the vast majority of disabled people, most of whom want a choice. When you look at the polls, you find that most of the population in the UK is in favour of some change in the law to allow assisted dying — it's around 80%. When you narrow it down to disabled groups, an even greater number support terminally ill people being given this choice. I'm disabled myself and I have been for the past six years.

Q After 18 months, your request for a judicial review was rejected by the British Supreme Court in 2018. We can imagine this was very frustrating — what impact did it have on your campaigning approach?

A I was very disillusioned at the end of that. Besides that cul-de-sac, I was always sympathetic to the position that you need to go down the parliamentary route. [Dignity in Dying] is now pursuing a parliamentary strategy and I'm actively involved in supporting the campaign. We recently did a Zoom meeting for MPs and [earlier last year] I won over my local MP, Daniel Kawczynski, who was fervently against assisted dying when I first met him. I wrote to him and we had a long correspondence until he eventually met with me and has since come out publicly on social media to say he supports me and the campaign, and will continue to support the campaign, which is at least something. We've still got quite a way to go [in the UK] — so many other countries, like New Zealand and Australia, as well as some states in the US, are well ahead of us.

"Assisted dying is not euthanasia, euthanasia is not on the table for the UK"

Ben Brooks-Dutton, *author of It's Not Raining, Daddy, It's Happy*, from an interview as part of *Lost for Words*, Royal London's 2020 exhibition in collaboration with RANKIN

"If you're trying to a someone who has los love, there's actually you can do. Just don't because they still nee and laugh"

o something for
t someone they
a million things
ignore them,
d to eat, drink

Interview with
Eimear McBride
Author

The acclaimed writer, whose father and brother died when they were young men, speaks about Irish funerary traditions and how they helped her come to terms with her loss

Having spent her childhood between County Sligo and County Mayo in Ireland, Eimear McBride moved to London in the 1990s. She initially trained as an actor before changing lanes to become a writer, and in her late twenties wrote her first book, *A Girl is a Half-formed Thing*, and realised her true calling in life. First published in 2013, her debut novel explores the relationship between a young woman and her brother who has a brain tumour; it earned her the Baileys Women's Prize for Fiction and the Goldsmiths Prize, and cemented her standing as one of Ireland's most exciting new writers. The book was dedicated to her brother, Donagh McBride, who died from a brain tumour when he was just 28. She has since released *The Lesser Bohemians*, which won the James Tait Black Memorial Prize, and *Strange Hotel*, which was received with great acclaim in 2020.

Q Tell us a bit about your background.

A I grew up in the west of Ireland. My parents were both nurses – my father was a psychiatric nurse. I had three brothers. When I was 17, I moved to London for drama school and then, when I was 27, I wrote *A Girl is a Half-formed Thing*, which took me nine years to get published. Since then I've written two more novels. I live in London and have done for pretty much all of my adult life, apart from a couple of years back in Cork.

Q You mentioned you came to London for drama school. Before your writing career, did you aspire to be an actor?

A After my father died when I was eight, my mother sent me to drama classes because she thought it would be good for me, and it was. I enjoyed showing off very much. That was my thing when I was a teenager.

Q That must have been hard to process at that age. Did you find that your early experience of loss changed your perception of death?

A It changes everything, because suddenly the world is finite. He died at home in our house, I watched him die. It wasn't something that was sanitised and away in a hospital, I saw him suffer and, in the Irish tradition, when he died he was laid out in the house. I saw and touched the dead body. It really changed my attitude to the body and the life of the body. You really know that it comes to an end – there's no sense of that feeling of being invincible that people seem to have when they're young, that somehow death doesn't touch them. When you lose someone young you don't have that protection.

Q What are some of the Irish traditions around death and mourning?

A It was very much that if you could die at home, you would die at home. At that point, in the mid-1980s, I don't know if there was any hospice care, especially not in rural Ireland. Because my mother was a nurse, she was able to do a lot of the care herself. [My father] died in the house, and, slightly macabre, his sister prepared the body herself, rather than a funeral director. All of that was done in the house, and then the funeral guys came and brought the coffin and he was laid out in the front room for two days. Everyone in the village came to pay their respects and offer their condolences. Everyone was brought in to have a look at him and have a cup of tea and a slice of cake, and talk about him. That was completely normal.

Q How much is that still practised?

A It's less common than it used to be. One of my brothers died 20 years ago, and he was also laid out in the house, but I think that, since then, it's become less common. It still does happen, though, and when the body is about to be taken to the church, they come and close the coffin and people carry it out of the house and walk with it before putting it into the hearse, and it goes to the church and stays there overnight for mass the next day.

Q Do you think that the Irish approach to death is helpful for family and friends of the deceased?

A I think it's very beneficial for the community at large and for the family if there's a public acknowledgement of your grief. Everyone knows what's happened and it's been acknowledged – that life has been spoken about and celebrated – so I think it's a really important thing.

Certainly, when I came [to England], I found it very odd how people die and then the relative disappears for a while and then comes back and no one really says anything about it. I do think that acknowledgement of the passing is a really important thing. After my brother died, I came back to England, as I had spent time nursing him in Ireland, and the number of people who never mentioned it at all was very, very odd.

Q Your first book tells the story of a pair of siblings where the brother has a brain tumour. Was that intentionally biographical and did the process of writing about it help you come to terms with your own loss?

A When I started to write the book, I was like, "I'll definitely not write about a girl losing her brother as that would be terrible and sentimental," and then of course found myself writing exactly that. While it isn't a memoir and it's not my brother's story, and that girl isn't me, it's a memorial, in a way, to that experience of having loved him and having gone through the loss of him, so that is truthful. I'm a bit anti the whole art and catharsis [thing]. I think it can be that for other people, but it certainly didn't feel like that for me.

Q Did you adopt any coping mechanisms for your loss?

A It was odd because I came back to London and I didn't have a job, so I was working as a temp. My first temp job was writing thank you cards to people [whose] family members had died from cancer and they had given donations rather than flowers, so that was very bizarre, but I was just so poor. I really needed that £6 an hour. My partner was working away and wasn't there, so I was alone a lot that first year. It was very hard, but in some ways useful, because it forced me through, there was no way around what was happening. I felt like I owed it to [my brother] to suffer the loss and go through it. He was 28 and he was dead, and the least I could do was mourn him, to go through that experience.

Q You've experienced a lot of loss in your life. Can you ever be fully prepared for it?

A I don't think so. Even when my brother died, I knew that he was dying so it wasn't a shock in the way that my father's death had been. I was 21, so I really knew what was happening, but when it happened, it still shattered me. It's really hard when it's someone who is young who hasn't really had a life, or a chance, someone who leaves nothing behind. The thing I found very hard was that there were

no children, he didn't have a house, there was no job that he left behind where he had made something. It was like he had just disappeared, and I think that is a harder type of grief than when someone old dies.

Q It is sometimes easier when someone has a legacy.

A I think that's why people are so obsessed with launching charities in people's names, because they want to create something lasting to memorialise that person's life. I dedicated *A Girl is a Half-formed Thing* to my brother and I felt very strongly that it had to be his full name. It was pre-internet, so that name didn't exist anywhere except on his gravestone.

Q How do you think that we can break the taboos surrounding death and loss?

A In a way I think that we have to start a step further back and acknowledge the importance of life and the body [we're in]. I think the unhelpful thing about the Irish experience is the legacy of Catholicism, which is always so geared to, "Oh, we will meet again in the afterlife, everything's going to be great next time around." And I think it's really important to acknowledge that, OK, maybe there is an afterlife, but we definitely know there is this life and we don't know anyone who has gone to the afterlife and come back. People are so set outside their own bodies but that doesn't help with the culture that we live in, which is obsessed with making women uncomfortable with their bodies and making them have impossible expectations. People don't feel like the life in their body is something to enjoy and celebrate unless they're a size 2. I think that separation between the body and the soul is really sad.

Q Lastly, do you think about your own death?

A All the time! Plus, I'm a hypochondriac so I really think about it a lot. I'm in my mid-forties now and it's on my mind more now that I'm probably at the halfway point, if I'm lucky. My husband and I have discussed it and we both know what the general plan is if one goes before the other, and obviously when you have a child you have to make plans. I don't find those practical things particularly difficult. I think that the [COVID-19 pandemic] has been quite interesting because people are being confronted with [mortality] a lot more than they ever have. I think the anti-mask brigade think they exist in some kind of fantasy world where death doesn't really happen, which is the problem with postmodernism generally – we think we can just argue our way out of anything, apparently. But you can't argue yourself out of death, and that's that!

"I felt like I owed it to [my brother] to suffer the loss and go through it. He was 28 and he was dead, and the least I could do was mourn him, to go through that experience"

Further resources

The grief that follows the loss of
a loved one can often feel like a deeply
personal and lonely journey, but sharing
bereavement can lighten the load.
Here is a list of information, guidance
and support helplines that can help
you to cope with bereavement

General information and guidance

Bereavement and counselling support in Ireland
Information on dealing with the death of a loved one can be found on Ireland's government advice portal.
citizensinformation.ie/en/death/bereavement_counselling_and_support/bereavement_counselling_andsupport_services.html

Grief after bereavement
This NHS guide to grief talks through the common symptoms and offers advice on grief management, as well as contacts for professional support.
nhs.uk/conditions/stress-anxiety-depression/coping-with-bereavement

Charities and support services

Bereavement Advice Centre
Offers practical information, advice and signposting on the many issues that people face after the death of a loved one.
Helpline (Mon-Fri, 9am-5pm; closed on bank holidays): 0800 634 9494.
bereavementadvice.org

Care for the Family
A charity providing help for those living with loss to deal with their grief and rebuild their lives.
careforthefamily.org.uk/family-life/bereavement-support

Cruse Bereavement Care
The UK's leading bereavement charity, which offers a support helpline and website with advice on coping with grief.
Helpline (Mon and Fri, 9.30am-5pm; Tue-Thu, 9.30am-8pm; weekends, 10am-2pm): 0808 808 1677.
cruse.org.uk

GriefChat
A free online messaging service for bereaved people to share their story with a qualified bereavement counsellor.
griefchat.co.uk

Irish Hospice Foundation
A charity that provides information and support for those dealing with the death of a loved one in Ireland. Offers a free bereavement support line.
Helpline (Mon-Fri, 10am-1pm): 1800 807077.
hospicefoundation.ie/bereavement-2-2

Marie Curie
Care, guidance and support for people living with and affected by terminal illnesses is provided by the charity. It provides a free helpline and online chat service to connect with others dealing with loss.
Helpline (Mon-Fri, 8am-6pm; Sat, 10-4pm): 0800 090 2309.
mariecurie.org.uk/help/support/bereaved-family-friends
Free online chat service: *community.mariecurie.org.uk*

National Grief Awareness Week
Organised by The Good Grief Trust, this is an annual campaign in the UK to raise awareness about grief and the support available.
nationalgriefawarenessweek.org

Samaritans
A 24-hour helpline that offers support for anyone going through a difficult time.
Helpline: 116123.
samaritans.org

The Good Grief Trust
A charity offering advice and support for all those affected by grief in the UK.
thegoodgrieftrust.org

Widowed & Young (WAY)
A national charity that provides bereavement support for people who are aged 50 or under when they lose their partner.
widowedandyoung.org.uk

Grief support for children

A list of organisations offering support for children and young people in the UK and Ireland who are dealing with the loss of a loved one.

Child Bereavement Network
A hub for those working with bereaved children, young people and their families across the UK to improve bereavement care for children.
childhoodbereavementnetwork.org.uk

Child Bereavement UK
Support for children and young people up to the age of 25, and their families, who are facing bereavement, as well as support for parents dealing with the loss of a child.
Helpline: 0800 028 8840.
childbereavementuk.org

Children's Grief Awareness Week
Founded by the charity Grief Encounter, this is an annual campaign that raises awareness of bereaved children and young people in the UK and the help that's available.
childrensgriefawarenessweek.com

Grief Encounter
A charity providing support for bereaved children and young people.
Helpline (Mon-Fri, 9am-9pm): 0808 802 0111.
griefencounter.org.uk

Hope Again
Cruse Bereavement Care's website that helps young people cope with living after loss.
hopeagain.org.uk

The Grief Network
A community by and for young people (those in their teens, twenties and thirties) affected by the loss of a loved one. It runs meet-ups in London where bereaved young people connect and share their stories of loss.
thegrief.network

The Irish Childhood Bereavement Network
A member organisation for those working with bereaved children and young people in Ireland.
childhoodbereavement.ie

Winston's Wish
A charity supporting children and young people after the death of a parent or sibling.
Helpline (Mon-Fri, 9am-5pm): 0808 802 0021.
winstonswish.org

YoungMinds Crisis Messenger
A free, 24/7 text support line for young people across the UK experiencing a mental health crisis. Text YM to 85258 to access the service.

Support for dealing with traumatic loss

A list of resources providing specific information, guidance and support for those who have lost a loved one through death from a traumatic situation, suicide, drug or alcohol use or accident.

Assist Trauma Care
A charity offering assistance, support and self-help for those dealing with traumatic loss such as death by homicide, or who have survived trauma.
assisttraumacare.org.uk/our-service/traumatic-bereavement

Bereaved through Alcohol and Drugs
A source of information and support for anyone who has lost a loved one as a result of drug or alcohol use.
beadproject.org.uk

Cruse Bereavement Care, traumatic loss
Information for people who have lost someone they care about in a disaster or traumatic situation.
cruse.org.uk/get-help/traumatic-bereavement/traumatic-loss

Facing the Future
Developed by the Samaritans and Cruse Bereavement Care, this is a support group for people bereaved by suicide.
facingthefuturegroups.org

Finding Your Way
Published by Ireland's PARC Road Safety Group, this is a guide for families in Ireland dealing with the loss or serious injury of a loved one through a road traffic collision.
parcroadsafety.ie/uploads/2/8/8/8/28885317/2019_edition.pdf

Help Is at Hand
An NHS guide to support people dealing with the death of a loved one by suicide.
www.nhs.uk/Livewell/Suicide/Documents/Help is at Hand.pdf

Support After Murder & Manslaughter
A UK charity supporting families bereaved by murder and manslaughter.
Helpline: 0121 472 2912.
samm.org.uk

Survivors of Bereavement by Suicide
Support for people over the age of 18 in the UK who have lost someone to suicide.
Helpline (Mon-Fri, 9am-9pm): 0300 111 5065.
uksobs.org

On death and loss
RANKIN

"The fact is, like birth we all have to die. The taboo around it is one of our own making and, therefore, one that we can break down ourselves"

How to Die Well is a pretty crazy title for a book but it's one I think the world needs. My journey to co-creating it started 15 years ago when my mum and dad passed away. Obviously, it was a shock.

For many of us, our parents are our safety nets and our shelter in the day-to-day. Without them, you no longer have that place to go to or the protection for that part of you that will always be a child. I just wasn't ready. I wasn't ready for the grief, I wasn't ready for the loss, and I wasn't ready to deal with my life without them. On top of that, I didn't really say goodbye properly. In every way, I felt completely unprepared.

This loss has stayed with me all of that time and it still creeps up on me at the most bizarre times: passing by a reflection I think is my dad and realising it's me or remembering a piece of advice my mum gave me in an interview. Their presence and the grief just doesn't go away and for me that is OK!

My parents dying and my total lack of understanding or knowledge about the subject made me want to help other people in the same situation and the idea of a self-help book came about. Let's be honest, most people are very scared of discussing death – I know I was. I think I was probably more scared of death than anyone, I couldn't imagine confronting my own mortality in any way and ultimately facing it left me paralysed with fear.

But the truth is, talking about the most difficult things in life makes living them so much easier. Although I don't think I'll ever not be scared of death, I've come to a point where I can live with it and certainly talk about it. The paralysis I once felt has gone and, in fact, I think I almost enjoy talking about it now. The more I discuss it, the more diluted the fear becomes.

The fact is, like birth we all have to die. The taboo around it is one of our own making and, therefore, one that we can break down ourselves. That is especially true when we are discussing death and all of the complicating things that surround it. Hopefully, this book goes some way to making this subject an easier one to discuss and understand.

Royal London was set up to work against funeral poverty and, for over 150 years, they've continued to support people in extreme, life-changing situations. So, when we were approached by them, I was confident we would be able to create a project that could help people in the purest form – and that's what we've tried to do.

In these times of COVID-19, death is something that's become reduced to numbers and data. It seems we're now even further away from the humanity in death that we need. Although we started this project before the pandemic, there is no doubt that it has even more resonance now.

Even today, 15 years on, curating this book has been incredibly powerful and very helpful for me. I hope that people use it to find positivity in this difficult subject matter and, after reading, are able to perhaps see death in a slightly warmer light.

Glossary

Adrenocorticotrophin (page 179)
The hormone that's released by the pituitary gland during the body's response to grief. It triggers a chemical reaction that releases the stress hormone cortisol.

All Souls' Day (page 73)
Practised predominantly by the Catholic church, All Souls' Day, marked annually on 2 November, commemorates the dead. On this day, people visit the graves of departed family members and pray for them, believing they will be released from purgatory into heaven.

Anticipatory grief (page 165)
A type of grief that starts before the death of a loved one after a terminal diagnosis has been given.

Capital acquisitions tax (page 31)
A form of tax relating to gifts and inheritance, which are tax-free up to a certain threshold. The level of tax depends on the relationship between the individuals giving and receiving the benefit.

Cardiopulmonary resuscitation (page 64)
Often referred to as CPR, cardiopulmonary resuscitation is an emergency procedure whereby an individual administers chest compressions to someone who is in cardiac arrest in order to maintain their brain function by restoring blood circulation and breathing. Chest compressions can be given rhythmically to the tune of "Stayin' Alive" by the Bee Gees.

Celebrant (pages 101, 113)
A person who leads an official, and often secular, ceremony, such as a funeral or wedding.

Complicated grief (pages 165, 169)
Also called persistent complex bereavement disorder, complicated grief is a severe and often debilitating emotional response to a loss that doesn't subside with time.

Cumulative grief (page 165)
A build-up of grief that can happen when multiple losses are suffered by a person either at the same time or within a short time frame; or a response to a death that triggers feelings about previous losses that perhaps weren't dealt with at the time.

Death Cafe (pages 146, 147, 148, 169)
Founded by Jon Underwood, a Death Cafe is a volunteer-run support group through which people come together to talk openly about death over cake and tea.

Delayed grief (page 165)
Often described as a sudden and overwhelming sadness, delayed grief may occur a few weeks, months or even years after the death of a loved one.

Digital legacy (pages 124, 129, 151)
The digital information about a person that's left behind online after their death, including social media profiles, videos, photos, gaming profiles and any personal websites.

Dirge (page 73)
A slow song of mourning or lament for the dead, often performed at funerals.

Embalming (pages 69, 78, 142)
A process where a chemical solution is introduced inside the body of someone who has recently died in order to slow down the decomposition process and preserve the body, giving the deceased a more restful appearance.

Epitaph (page 132)
Rooted in the Greek word *epitaphios* – *epi* meaning "at" or "over", and *taphos* meaning "tomb" – an epitaph is a short text or poem in memory of somebody who has died, often inscribed on their gravestone.

Eulogy (pages 84, 113)
A eulogy is either a written passage or speech that pays homage to a person who has recently died. While a eulogy is commonly read at a funeral, it can also appear in news publications.

Executor (pages 17, 19, 20, 27, 28, 31, 151)
A named individual whose duty is to carry out the instructions written in a will.

Hospice movement (pages 32, 136, 137)
A term that applies to the evolution of end-of-life and palliative care services in the UK over the past 50 years. The modern hospice movement emerged in the late 1960s with the establishment of St Christopher's Hospice in London by Dame Cicely Saunders.

Intestate (page 28)
A term applied to those who die without making a will.

Letter of wishes (pages 17, 19)
A document that normally accompanies a will. While it's not legally binding, it provides advice on how the deceased would like their estate to be dealt with.

Living will (pages 19, 55, 114)
Also known as an advance decision, this legal document is a written statement of what medical care a person would like to receive if they're unable to express their wishes because of a terminal illness or being unconscious for an extended period.

Mevlit (page 73)
A Turkish mourning ceremony held after somebody's death and burial. Passages from the Qur'an are usually recited, and family and friends gather in a circle and share sweets and drinks while remembering their loved one.

Neuroplasticity (page 179)
A process that can be triggered by bereavement whereby the brain rewires itself, creating new pathways that prioritise primitive functions — survival instincts over decision-making.

Palliative care (pages 32, 108, 134, 135, 136, 137, 151, 152, 177, 207)
A form of care for the terminally ill that's intended to make the final years, weeks or months of life as comfortable and dignified as possible, with a focus on pain management and psychological or spiritual support.

Power of attorney (pages 19, 55, 56)
A legal document granting a trusted friend or family member the power to make decisions on your behalf, should you become incapacitated.

Probate (pages 9, 31, 51, 54, 57, 162, 185)
The financial and legal process of sorting out someone's estate after they pass away, normally settling any debts and distributing assets in accordance with the deceased's will.

Psalms of lament (page 170)
A collection of poems and hymns, found in the holy books of both Christianity and Judaism, that express sorrow in response to human struggle. They include community laments, which deal with situations of collective crisis, and individual laments, which tackle isolated problems.

Public health funeral (pages 67, 87, 141, 142)
A no-frills funeral that's organised by a person's local council if they die in poverty with no next of kin, or if the family of the individual are unable or unwilling to pay for a funeral.

Requiem Mass (page 70)
A type of Catholic funeral that involves blessing the coffin with holy water. There are recitals from the Bible by the family and priest, as well as the offering of Holy Communion.

Residence nil rate band (page 31)
Intended to make it easier to pass on the family home to children or grandchildren, the residence nil rate band applies to those whose personal estate exceeds the inheritance tax threshold. In this scenario, if you are giving your home to your descendants, you may gain an additional threshold before inheritance tax is due.

Shroud (pages 81, 83)
Also called a burial sheet, a shroud is a piece of fabric that's used to cover the body before burial.

Sraddha (page 170)
A Hindu ceremony that remembers and honours the dead. Performed by the male descendant of the deceased in the days following their death and on the death anniversary, the Sraddha rites are thought to protect the spirits of the dead and their ancestors in their journey to the higher realms. Sraddha is also performed collectively in the autumn during Pitru Paksha, the fortnight of the ancestors.

How to Die Well: A Practical Guide to Death, Dying and Loss, spearheaded by Royal London and published by RANKIN

First published in the UK in 2021
Rankin Publishing Ltd
110-114 Grafton Road
London NW5

Editor
Natasha Stallard

Sub-editor
Sam Nicholls

Art direction
SEA

Illustrator
Andrea Ucini

Contributors
Flora Baker, Dino Bonacic, Ryan Cahill, Vanita
James, Amita Joshi, Ella Kenny, Dr Kathryn Mannix,
Barry O'Dwyer, Rankin, Rhik Samadder, Natalie
Shooter, Ramsay Short, Kevin Toolis, Megan Wallace,
Ava Williams

Print management
&Printed

Thanks to
The Abernethy-Hope family, Ahmed Alsisi, Malin
Andersson, Jeff Brazier, Ben Brooks-Dutton, Ellie
Brown, Noel Conway, Laura Cooper, Divina De Campo,
Samantha Dixon, Amy Downes, Maks Fus-Mickiewicz,
Gloria Hunniford, Konnie Huq, Eimear McBride, Judith
Moran, Charlie Phillips, Roisin Rennell, Ben Buddy
Slack, John Stapleton, Carole Walford, Louise Winter,
Hasina Zaman

A catalogue record of this book is available from the
British Library.

ISBN 978-0-9955741-7-5